MODERN GREEK FOLKLORE

GARLAND FOLKLORE BIBLIOGRAPHIES
(General Editor: Alan Dundes)
Vol. 9

GARLAND REFERENCE LIBRARY
OF THE HUMANITIES
Vol. 451

Garland Folklore Bibliographies

General Editor
Alan Dundes
University of California, Berkeley

MODERN GREEK FOLKLORE
An Annotated Bibliography

Julia E. Miller

GARLAND PUBLISHING, INC. • NEW YORK & LONDON
1985

Library of Congress Cataloging-in-Publication Data

Miller, Julia E., 1951–
  Modern Greek folklore.

  (Garland folklore bibliographies ; vol. 9) (Garland
reference library of the humanities ; vol. 451)
  Includes index.
    1. Folklore—Greece—Bibliography.   2. Greece—Social
life and customs—Bibliography.   3. Folk literature,
Greek—History and criticism—Bibliography.   I. Title.
II. Series: Garland folklore bibliographies ; v. 9.
III. Series: Garland reference library of the humanities ;
v. 451.
Z5984.G8M54   1985   [GR170]   016.398′09495   83-48283
ISBN 0-8240-9038-1 (alk. paper)

Printed on acid-free, 250-year-life paper
Manufactured in the United States of America

ACKNOWLEDGMENTS

I developed an interest in modern Greece when I was a Classics major at Kenyon College and while studying and traveling in Greece and Cyprus during the summer of 1972. William E. McCulloh, Professor of Classics at Kenyon College, encouraged and supported me.

At the University of Pennsylvania I began folklore studies in order to make scholarly application of my interest in modern Greek culture. This bibliography began as an independent study for Henry Glassie of Penn's Department of Folklore and Folklife. Faculty support also came from Dan Ben-Amos and Kenneth Goldstein.

The staff of the Interlibrary Loan Department at Van Pelt Library, University of Pennsylvania, located and acquired books and articles for this work. Colleagues in Van Pelt's Reference Department who assisted with translation problems are Joan Anderson, Jane Bryan, and Russ Chenoweth. Ellen DeMarinis provided moral support, assuring me that I would finish the bibliography some day.

Special thanks are due to my husband, James W. Vick, who encouraged me to complete this project when family affairs seemed to prevent it, who got the computer to produce a workable format, and who took on many additional hours of child care, all without complaint.

CONTENTS

EDITOR'S PREFACE

The Garland Folklore Bibliographies are intended to provide ready access to the folklore scholarship of a particular country or area or to the scholarship devoted to a specific folklore genre or theme. The annotations are designed to be informative and evaluative so that prospective readers may have some idea of the nature and worth of the bibliographical items listed. No bibliography is ever complete and all bibliographies are doomed to become obsolete almost immediately upon publication as new monographs and articles appear. Still, there is no substitute for a comprehensive, intelligently annotated bibliography for anyone desiring to discover what has been written on a topic under investigation.

Folklore is to be found in every country and culture in the world. The size of the country turns out not always to be a reliable index of the amount of folklore scholarship devoted to that country's traditions. Often, it is relatively smaller countries, perhaps in part attributable to strong feelings of national identity among its citizens and scholars, which on a purely per-capita basis have contributed more to international folkloristics than larger, more populous countries. So we find that Finland, Hungary, and Ireland have produced a disproportionate number of folklorists, not to mention recorded folklore texts.

Greece is a good example of a small country with a strong tradition of folklore scholarship. However, folklorists there have labored under the heavy burden of "the glory that was Greece" in ancient times. For that matter, classical Greek culture continues to dominate elitist education throughout the Western world. It is unthinkable to study philosophy and drama without reference to the likes of Aristotle, Plato, and Sophocles. Because of the long-standing penchant among intellectuals to worship classical Greece, both in Greece and elsewhere, there has been some reluctance to study so-called "Modern Greek" culture, the feeling being that modern Greek folklore cannot possibly compare with the greatness of classical creations. Indeed, one of the main motivations for collecting and studying modern Greek folklore was to discover whether any vestigial remains from the ancient past might still survive among contemporary Greek peasants. In view of the unique and hallowed aura which surrounds Greek classical civilization, it is quite understandable that so many of the folklorists carrying out research in modern Greek folklore eschewed most of the theories and methods available, preferring instead to concentrate upon attempting to trace various items back to presumed parallel forms, if not actual precursors, in antiquity.

Because of the centrality of ancient Greek culture among the educated throughout the Western world, the content of modern Greek folklore is surely of special significance. Yet since so few folklorists possess a reading knowledge of modern Greek, much of the published data is inaccessible. The inability to decipher the Greek alphabet or, more specifically, the spoken language has even been immortalized since the sixteenth century through the traditional metaphor of something being "Greek to me." This linguistic lacuna has also tended to discourage folklore fieldwork in Greece by non-Greeks except by a select group of dedicated scholars who acquired the requisite expertise.

In this context, folklorists everywhere will surely have reason to be grateful to Julia E. Miller for having compiled *Modern Greek Folklore: An Annotated Bibliography* which includes scholarship by Greek and non-Greek scholars. Born in State College, Pennsylvania, into an academic family, Julia Miller grew up in Arlington and Belmont, Massachusetts. At Kenyon College, she earned her B.A. in classics in 1973. It was during her undergraduate years that she first became acquainted with modern Greek. On an archaeological dig in Cyprus in the summer of 1972, she became more and more intrigued by contemporary rather than classical Greek culture. After receiving a Master's degree in Library Science from Simmons College in 1975, Julie Miller entered the graduate program in Folklore and Folklife at the University of Pennsylvania. Her M.A. in that program was awarded in 1984. Her dual training in folklore and library science, combined with her fascination with modern Greek culture, led to the present bibliographic project. Since 1976, she has served as a reference librarian in the main library of the University of Pennsylvania. Whether one is curious about modern Greek folklore in general or a single genre or theme in particular, e.g., the lament or the firewalking ritual of the Anastenaria, this survey of books and articles should prove indispensable. To "the glory that *was* Greece" we must add all the marvelous folklore that *is* still to be found in contemporary Greek life. We must not let our justified admiration for classical Greece prevent us from exploring further the exciting possibilities of the folklore of the modern period.

Alan Dundes, Editor
Garland Folklore Bibliography Series

FOREWORD

Scope and Nature of the Bibliography

This work lists and annotates books, articles, dissertations, and published conference papers on modern Greek folklore. Greek folklore is treated as a cultural, not geographic, phenomenon. Therefore, works on folklore of Greece and Cyprus, as well as Greek-American and Greek-Canadian folklore are included.

This bibliography includes works which add to our knowledge of modern Greek folklore by describing, summarizing, or analyzing Greek folklore material and events. Although theoretical studies are more valued today, descriptive works are often the only data available for some topics. An eyewitness account may be the sole record of a ritual no longer practiced or radically changed and can be analyzed for comparison with more recent forms. In other instances little is available on particular subjects, e.g., folkdance, and, therefore, quasi-scholarly works that include historical and ethnographic data are listed. Ethnographies are not listed here unless they include significant discussion or description of folklore.

The modern nation of Greece emerged in 1821 with the War of Independence. The entries in this bibliography cover a time period from mid-nineteenth century to 1983. With a few exceptions, I have examined every item. Materials cited are written in English, French, German, Greek and Italian. Greek titles are transliterated and translated.

Since the authors of the works listed here have used various transliteration schemes and there does not appear to be an optimum one, I simply have tried to be consistent and use either well-known forms or the phonemic transliteration recommended by the Modern Greek Studies Association (*MGSA Bulletin* 16(1):

6–7). Greek authors who wrote in more than one language are identified with an English transliteration of their names. No bibliography is ever complete. I have attempted to list works on Greek folklore that are significant and contribute to an understanding of the field. For some Greek authors, only the most important works in Greek are included. Some of these authors are very prolific, and their other works can be found in the bibliographies listed at the end of the Introduction.

Organization and Form of Entries

This bibliography combines studies, survey articles, and bibliographies in one alphabetical listing by author's name. An index provides access by subject. A shorter classified version of this bibliography appeared in *Modern Greek Society: A Social Science Newsletter* 7(1): 13–48, 1979.

I have used a modified form of the *Journal of American Folklore* style for entries. For older or translated books, I have listed readily available editions with date, place, and publisher of the original indicated in parentheses. Annotations are mainly descriptive.

INTRODUCTION

The history of Greek folklore studies is well documented in Michael Herzfeld's *Ours Once More: Folklore, Ideology, and the Making of Modern Greece* (Austin, University of Texas Press, 1982). Study of folklore was significant in that country's quest for nationhood. After independence from Turkey in 1821, Greeks needed to prove to European powers that they were not only worthy of statehood but of realizing their dream, the *Megali Idhea* [Great Idea]: of restoring to Greece all of the Greek-speaking world, including Constantinople and Asia Minor. Furthermore, some European scholars, in particular a widely respected German historian, J.F. Fallmerayer, accused the Greeks of being genetically Slavs and Turks. Using ethnographic data, Fallmerayer claimed that centuries of occupation and intermarriage had long ago weakened and destroyed the blood of the original Hellenes.

To prove that they were the true descendants of ancient Hellas and to fight Fallmerayer's accusation, Greek scholars used ethnographic data. Since they saw folklore as the only living survival of an earlier time, the development of national identity was based on examination of all aspects of traditional culture: poetry, songs, tales, art, customs, and traditional beliefs and practices. This was such an important national priority that in 1856 Parliament began to provide funds for folklore research.

The study of ethnology and comparative religion flourished in Europe in the late nineteenth and early twentieth centuries. English and German scholars visited Greece and wrote about modern poetry, music, religious practices, and customs, many of them finding similarities with antiquity. These works were widely read by non-Greeks and helped sway the foreign intelligentsia to Greece's cause.

One Greek scholar in particular was responsible for organizing research activity into a discipline which employed strict Euro-

pean methodology and for giving it a name. In 1884, Nikolaos
Politis (1852–1921) coined the word "laographia." In 1909 he
founded the Greek Folklore Society [Elleniki Laographiki
Hetairea] and published the first volume of the Society's journal,
Laographia, that same year. Politis established a cross-cultural
perspective as well as an ancient Greek vs modern Greek perspective. He also emphasized the importance of studying actual
customs and folklife, not just texts.

The work of Politis and his students helped the non-Greek
world slowly accept the idea of the modern Greeks' descent from
the original Hellenes. As Herzfeld states, the sense of "cultural
continuity with Greece, the European character of the entire
Greek people, and the territorial and chronological boundaries of
Hellenism" (p. 121) was largely developed by folklorists like Politis. As acceptance grew, so did the fervor for the *Megali Idhea*.

However, due to internal administrative problems, Greece lost
support of the Allies. In 1922, the Turks burned the large Greek-
speaking city of Smyrna, the Greek army returned home defeated
and thousands of Greek-speaking refugees fled to Greece. It was
also a catastrophe for folklore studies. Politis died and his discipline became a mere academic concern, losing its political focus.

With the influx of immigrants, research societies were formed
to study and perpetuate their culture, as well as to preserve and
reproduce their traditional crafts. A popular arts movement began in 1921 when expositions were organized to display traditional arts. The Greek Anthropology Society [Elleniki An-
thropologiki Hetairea] was founded in 1924, and the Benaki
Museum of ethnography, history and folklore, in 1931.

Politis' student Stilpon Kyriakides (1887–1964) carried on his
work and developed new areas of folklore research. Although he
did many survivalist studies, he stressed that folklore not only
study the past, but must examine the contemporary life of the
people. The University of Thessaloniki was opened in 1926 and
he became its professor of folklore. He founded the Folklore
Archives of the University of Thessaloniki in 1927.

Kyriakides' student, Giorgios A. Megas (1893–1976) became
director of the Folklore Archives in 1936 and began publishing its
annual in 1939. In 1947 Megas assumed the folklore chair at the
University of Athens. Megas emphasized the importance of

studying the psychic and spiritual world of the people and was a leader in folktale research.

Other important Greek academics who followed Megas in studying folklore are Giorgios Spyridakis (1906–1975), Demetrios Petropoulos (1906–1979), Demetrios Loukatos, Stephen Imellos, Alke Kyriakiou-Nestoros, and Gregory Gizelis. Their academic institutions are the Universities of Athens, Thessaloniki, and Ioannina. There are folklore archives at all three universities. In addition to those included in this bibliography, many more works in Greek by these and other folklorists can be found by consulting the following sources:

Bibliographia tes Ellenikes Laographias
  [Bibliography of Greek Folklore] in:
  Laographia X for 1910–20
  Epeteris tou Laographikou Archeiou [Annals of the Folklore Archives. Academy of Athens] V, VII, IX–X, XI–XII, XIII–XIV for 1921–61

Additional sources are:

Most volumes of *Laographia* include bibliographies of folklore works published that year. Some volumes of *Laographia* include summaries of its articles *in French.*
Bulletin Analytique de Bibliographie Hellénique, Institut Français d'Athènes, 1946– . Includes descriptive annotation *in French* for many entries.
Internationale Volkskundliche Bibliographie, Bonn: R. Habelt, 1917– .
Univ. of Cincinnati. Library. *Catalog of the Modern Greek Collection,* Boston: G.K. Hall, 1978.

Many non-Greeks have contributed to the study of Greek folklore and, later, Greek-American folklore. Classicists from Oxford and Cambridge are Richard M. Dawkins, John Cuthbert Lawson, W.H.D. Rouse. Some important European scholars are Margaret Alexiou, S. Baud-Bovy, Roderick Beaton, Melpo Merlier. In America Dorothy D. Lee, and, more recently, Anna Caraveli, Loring M. Danforth, Robert Georges, Michael Herzfeld, Robert Teske should be cited.

Data for this introduction came from:

Herzfeld, Michael. *Ours Once More: Folklore, Ideology and the Making of Greece*. Austin: University of Texas, 1982.

Loukatos, Demetrios. Etat actuel des études folkloriques en Grèce. *Actes du IIe Congrès Internationale des Etudes du Sud-Est Européen, Athènes, 7–3 Mai, 1970*. A: 551–582.

Modern Greek Folklore

001 Anonymous
   1835. Popular Superstitions of Greece.
   FRASER'S MAGAZINE 11: 218-225.

   This article describes beliefs in the
   supernatural as seen in older works,
   particularly a tract by Allatius (Cologne,
   1645) and the songs published by Claude
   Fauriel in 1825.

002 Anonymous
   1897. Folk Songs and Tales from Modern Greece.
   POET-LORE 9: 353-366.

   Text of seven songs from islands and the
   mainland and text of three tales with brief
   discussion make up this collectanea.

003 Abbott, G.F.
   1900. SONGS OF MODERN GREECE. Cambridge,
   England: University Press. 307 pp.

   A collection of modern Greek songs published
   in western Europe for the first time. The
   songs are arranged in two major groupings and
   further subdivided: 1) Heroic Poetry includes
   Historic ballads and Choral songs; 2) Romantic
   Poetry includes Idylls and love songs, Dancing
   songs, Miscellaneous, and Distichs. Each major
   section has an introduction. For each of the
   forty-nine songs and the distichs as a whole,
   Abbott provides commentary, the Greek text,
   English translation, and notes. Many of the
   songs were personally collected by the author.

004 Abbott, G.F
   1903. MACEDONIAN FOLKLORE. Hetaireia
   Makedonikon Spoudon. Hidryma Meleton
   Chersonesou tou Haimou. Ekdoseis, 100.
   Cambridge, England: University Press. 372 pp.

This book is the result of the author's
research in Macedonia between 1900-1901. The
material is arranged in nineteen chapters and
covers such areas as calendar customs and
festivities, divination, rites of passage,
spells, mythology, legends and riddles. Many
of the songs, tales, riddles and rhymes are
given in Greek with an English translation.
Detailed notes and a subject index provide
access to this rich collection as well as
references for further study.

005 Ahrens, Christian
    1973. Polyphony in Touloum Playing by the
    Pontic Greeks. YEARBOOK OF THE INTERNATIONAL
    FOLK MUSIC COUNCIL 5: 122-131.

    The touloum is a bagpipe-like instrument
    played by the Pontic Greeks. Ahrens describes
    its physical appearance, sound, and how it is
    made, held and played. Examples of touloum
    music are given.

006 Alevizos, Susan and Ted Alevizos
    1968. FOLKSONGS OF GREECE. New York: Oak
    Publishing. 96 pp.

    A collection of klephtic and historic songs,
    songs from the mainland and the islands,
    holiday songs, love songs and dances. For
    each song there is a history and description,
    the score with notations for guitar, and the
    Greek lyrics with transliteration and English
    translation.

007 Alexiou, Margaret B.
    1974. THE RITUAL LAMENT IN GREEK TRADITION.
    London: Cambridge University Press. 274 pp.

    This book studies the lament as it is found in

Greek literature, folklore, and ritual from
antiquity to the present. Part 1 describes
the lament and its development throughout the
ages. Part 2 classifies and analyzes the
different kinds of laments which include those
for the dead, for gods and heroes, and for the
destruction or fall of cities.
Some of this work is based on Alexiou's
fieldwork in Greece in 1963 and 1966. The
relationship between lamentation and ritual is
examined to understand why and how laments
have survived in the vernacular. In addition
to a general subject index, an index of motifs
and images is provided.

008 Alexiou, Margaret
    1975. The Lament of the Virgin in Byzantine
    Literature and Modern Greek Folk-Song.
    BYZANTINE AND MODERN GREEK STUDIES 1: 111-140.

    Laments of the Virgin can be found in Greek
    tradition from the sixth century to the
    present. This article examines the different
    types of laments including specific features
    of various versions found in modern folk
    tradition.

009 Alexiou, Margaret
    1978. Modern Greek Folklore and its Relation
    to the Past: the Evolution of Charos in Greek
    Tradition. In THE "PAST" IN MEDIEVAL AND
    MODERN GREEK CULTURE, ed.Speros Vryonis, jr.
    pp.221-236. Malibu: Undena Publications.

    The three figures of death in antiquity
    --Hades, Thanatos, and Charon--fused together
    to become Charos of modern popular tradition.
    Charos is known in folksongs and folk
    tradition as the agent of death. Alexiou uses
    Charos as an example of a survival in
    examining why some attitudes and beliefs
    persist, and why the figure of Charos, in

- 3 -

particular, is an adaptable tradition.

010 Alexiou, Margaret
1983. Sons, Wives and Mothers: Reality and
Fantasy in Some Modern Greek Ballads. JOURNAL
OF MODERN GREEK STUDIES 1: 73-111.

In this article, Alexiou analyzes five ballads
that have marriage and mother/son/daughter/or
daughter-in-law relationships as central
themes. She attempts to answer questions
relating the songs to social reality and
attitudes toward the values expressed in
them. This examination finds that the ballads
function to act out some of the tensions in
Greek rural life as well as to reconcile women
to their powerless status. Texts of the
ballads in Greek and English translation are
included.

011 Antoniades, Anne Gault
1954. THE ANASTENARIA: THRACIAN FIREWALKING
FESTIVAL. Athens: Society of Thracian Studies,
Publication 36. 22 pp.

This pamphlet is based on the author's
observation of the Anastenaria, a ritual
involving possession by the spirit of
St.Constantine, as seen in 1953 in the village
of Langada (near Salonika), as well as
discussion with the ritual's participants, the
Anastenarides. She describes the sacrifice of
the bull, the firewalkers' procession, and the
firewalking ritual. The evolution of this
complex ritual, the significance of the bull,
and the process of becoming an Anastenaris are
examined.

012 Antoniades, Sophia
1937. Le mouvement folkloriste en Grèce. FOLK
1: 94-97.

This brief history of the study of Greek
folklore documents the relationship between
the evolution Greek statehood and the
development of formal folklore study. The
most significant European and Greek scholars
are indicated as well as the activities of the
various folklore societies and research
centers.

013 Argenti, Philip P. and H.J.Rose
    1949. THE FOLKLORE OF CHIOS. Cambridge,
    England: University Press. 2 vols. 1199 pp.

    The authors described their work as "to the
    best of our knowledge, the first
    anthropological survey of a definite region of
    modern Greece"(p.1027). It is a collection of
    folklore and details of daily life on the
    island of Chios in the early 1940s. The
    material is exhaustively presented in sixteen
    chapters and eleven appendices. Areas covered
    include superstitions, calendar customs, rites
    of passage, folk medicine, folktales,
    folksongs, proverbs, riddles, sayings and
    games. Detailed descriptions of daily life,
    dress, and occupations are also provided.
    Song texts are in Greek and English.

014 Argenti, Philip P.
    1953. THE COSTUMES OF CHIOS; THEIR DEVELOPMENT
    FROM THE XVTH TO THE XXTH CENTURY. London:
    Batsford. 338 pp.

    This encyclopedic study of Chian costume is
    based on "documentation at its disposal"
    (p.1), and is by a diplomat who authored or
    edited more than ten works on Chios. The first
    part covers general information on Chian
    costume including, fabrics, dyes, accessories
    and stitching. The second and third parts are
    on men's clothing from the fifteenth century

to 1933 and women's clothing from the
sixteenth century to 1933, respectively.
Regional costumes are described in detail.
The book is illustrated with 119 plates (most
are colored) and 207 figures.

015 Argenti, Philip P.
1978. THE RELIGIOUS MINORITIES OF CHIOS: JEWS
AND ROMAN CATHOLICS. Cambridge, England:
University Press. 581 pp.

This historical study of two minorities of
Chios includes data on customs and religious
practices.

016 Arnott, Margaret Louise
1953. FOLK CUSTOMS SURROUNDING THE GREAT DAYS
OF EASTER IN GREECE. M.A. thesis. Hartford
Seminary Foundation. 134 pp.

Based on communication and correspondence with
Greeks, and on library research, this thesis
examines folk traditions surrounding the four
most important days of Holy Week: Great
Thursday, Good Friday, Great Saturday, and
Easter. The appendix includes first-hand
accounts of the Good Friday procession and the
Easter celebration for various years.

017 Arnott, Margaret Louise
1964. Bread for the Dead. ACTES DE VIE CONGRES
INTERNATIONAL DES SCIENCES ANTHROPOLOGIQUE ET
ETHNOLOGIQUES, PARIS, 30 JUILLET-6 AOUT 1960.
Tome II, pp.136-139. Paris: Musée de L'Homme.

This study of the roles bread and wheat play
commemorating the dead, traces pagan and
Christian practices to the present.

018 Arnott, Margaret L.

1971. Comments. CURRENT ANTHROPOLOGY 12 (1): 27.

Following a lengthy bibliographic essay on the studies of crisis cults, Arnott suggests that the Anastenaria is a crisis cult which began in the thirteenth century. She indicates the existence of a body of material on the Anastenaria in the Thracian Archives in Athens.

019 Arnott, Margaret L.
1971. Ethnographic Food Habits Research in Greece. ETHNOLOGIA EUROPAIA 5: 204-210.

This mainly descriptive article lists the kinds of food consumed in Greece today and mentions use of certain foods in ritual. Scholarship in Greek foodways is discussed.

020 Arnott, Margaret Louise
1975. The Breads of Mani. In GASTRONOMY: THE ANTHROPOLOGY OF FOOD AND FOOD HABITS, ed.Margaret L.Arnott. pp.297-304. The Hague: Mouton.

This article describes the making and function of breads from the region of Mani, including breads for Christmas, St. Basil's Day, Easter and Names Days. Includes photographs of breads.

021 Baggally, John W.
1968. GREEK HISTORICAL FOLKSONGS: THE KLEPHTIC BALLADS IN RELATION TO GREEK HISTORY (1715-1821). Chicago: Argonaut. 109 pp. (Original: Oxford University Press, 1936.)

This book provides English translation of twenty-eight klephtic ballads selected by the author from existing collections, mainly from

the nineteenth century. The commentary with
each ballad deals with historic accuracy. The
author does not find them to be valuable
sources for historical research but useful for
understanding the people of the time. The
introduction describes the history of the
klephts and their activities. A bibliography
of ballad collections and historical works is
included.

022 Barb, A.A.
1954. A Greek Serpent Ritual of Modern Times.
FOLKLORE 65: 48-49.

A description of a serpent festival in a
Kephalonian village, this article actually
summarizes a 1952 article by Loukatos.

023 Baud-Bovy, S.
1935-1938. CHANSONS DU DODECANESE, I-II.
Athens: Sideris. 2 vols. 391 pp., 466 pp.

Only the introduction, which includes
discussion of lyrics, instruments and rhythm,
is in French. For each of the Dodecanese
islands are wedding songs, women's songs,
religious songs, distichs and dance songs.
The text and words to songs are in Greek.

024 Baud-Bovy, Samuel
1936. LA CHANSON POPULAIRE GRECQUE DU
DODECANESE, I. LES TEXTES. Geneva: A.Kundig.
403 pp.

The thesis of Samuel Baud-Bovy, a Swiss
musicologist whose contribution to Greek folk
music scholarship is enormous, examines three
aspects of folksongs from thirteen Dodecanese
islands: 1) verse and the relationships
between poetic and musical rhythm, 2) text of
narrative songs, and 3) the distich. The

- 8 -

introduction refers to a forthcoming second
volume of musicological study which appears to
have never been published.

025 Baud-Bovy, Samuel
    1950. Sur la strophe de la chanson
    "cleftique." ANNUAIRE DE L'INSTITUT DE
    PHILOLOGIE ET D'HISTOIRE ORIENTALES ET SLAVES
    10: 53-78.

    In comparing klephtic songs from Crete, other
    islands and Asia Minor, Baud-Bovy finds that
    each strophe corresponds to a specific number
    of syllables. Includes seventy-five songs in
    Greek and French.

026 Baud-Bovy, Samuel
    1958. ETUDES SUR LA CHANSON CLEFTIQUE.
    Collection de l'Institut Français d'Athènes
    53. Athens: Institut Français d'Athènes. 125
    pp.

    The Klephts were guerilla fighters for Greek
    independence from mid-fifteenth century to
    1821 in central and northwestern Greece. In
    this ethnomusicological study melody and text
    of Klephtic songs from Roumely and Morea are
    examined. The author compares songs with and
    without refrains, contrasts some melodies to
    French tunes, and studies the influence of
    Balkan songs on the Klephtic ballads.

027 Baud-Bovy, Samuel
    1968. L'Evolution d'un chanson grecque.
    JOURNAL OF THE INTERNATIONAL FOLK MUSIC
    COUNCIL 20: 39-47.

    This examination of similarities and
    differences of Greek folk music with European
    music includes examples of parts of songs from
    various regions of Greece compared with

European songs.

028 Baud-Bovy, Samuel
1971. Chansons d'Epire du Nord et du Pont.
YEARBOOK OF THE INTERNATIONAL FOLK MUSIC
COUNCIL 3: 120-127.

This article discusses the similar repertories
of songs in Northern Epirus, near Albania,
with those from Pontus, in Asia Minor.
Bilingualism and a musical instrument are
elements of influence for each group of songs.

029 Baud-Bovy, Samuel
1972. CHANSONS POPULAIRES DE CRETE
OCCIDENTALE. Geneva: Minkoff. 310 pp.

A highly detailed and important study of
songs, called rizitika, from the western part
of Crete, this book is based on recordings
collected in 1930 and 1954. These songs are
traditionally sung by men and are not
accompanied by instruments. The book is
accompanied by a record of six songs. Texts
of songs are in Greek with French
translations.

030 Baud-Bovy, Samuel
1972. Sur une Chanson de Danse Balkanique.
REVUE DE MUSICOLOGIE 58: 153-161.

A musicological study of the music of the
Tsakonikos dance found in the Pelopennesus,
this article shows that although originally
foreign, the dance became Greek over the
centuries.

031 Beaton, Roderick
1980. FOLK POETRY OF MODERN GREECE. Cambridge,
England: University Press. 229 pp.

This comprehensive examination of Greek
folksong is based on research in Greece from
1974 to 1977. Beaton attempts to define the
demotic tradition, then examines the formula,
imagery and themes, development and function.
The final three chapters are devoted to the
poet, composition, and the effect of writing
on oral tradition. Examples of many songs in
both Greek and English are given. The book
includes an extensive bibliography as well as
a detailed subject index.

032 Beaton, Roderick
    1981. Was Digenes Akrites an Oral Poem?
    BYZANTINE AND MODERN GREEK STUDIES 7: 7-27.

    Beaton reviews the debate on the origin of the
    poem of "Digenes Akrites," discusses formula
    and subject, and concludes that although it
    may not have been "composed in performance,"
    versions of it were probably transmitted
    orally and its subject came from popular
    tradition.

033 Beaton, Roderick
    1982-83. Realism and Folklore in
    Nineteenth-Century Greek Fiction. BYZANTINE
    AND MODERN GREEK STUDIES 8: 103-122.

    This article studies the relationship between
    literary realism and folklore, and its effect
    on the emerging modern Greek identity. The
    focus especially concerns the work of Vikelas,
    Vizyinos and Papadiamandis, and how their
    fiction helped Greeks define themselves.
    Beaton finds that the growth and development
    of both modern Greek literature and folklore
    as a science were interwoven.

034 Becker, M.J.

1978. The Accuracy of Oral Tradition. Legends of Richard B.Seager, an American Archaeologist in Crete. INDIANA FOLKLORE 11: 175-191.

This article studies legends about an American archaeologist who died in Crete in 1925, collected in 1973 from non-literate people in north central Crete.

035 Bent, J.Theodore
1884. Some Games Played by Modern Greeks. FOLKLORE JOURNAL 2: 57-59.

The author, a writer and archaeologist, describes five games he saw played on the island of Samos.

036 Bent, James Theodore
1885. CYCLADES; OR LIFE AMONG THE INSULAR GREEKS. London: Longmans. 501 pp.

This account of a two-year trip in the Cyclades in the late nineteenth century includes many descriptions of customs, rituals and daily life.

037 Bent, J.Theodore
1885-1886. On Insular Greek Customs. JOURNAL OF THE ANTHROPOLOGICAL INSTITUTE OF GREAT BRITAIN AND IRELAND 15: 391-401.

A melange of customs from the Aegean Islands which Bent considers to be the richest field for the study of survivals. Included are life-cycle customs, descriptions of feast days, and descriptions of personification of natural phenomena that the author collected in mountain villages in forty islands visited over a period of three winters. An appendix by Mrs.Bent describes items she collected.

038 Bent, J.Theodore
    1888. The Three Evils of Destiny. LIVING AGE
    176: 410-418.

    This article describes beliefs and practices
    concerning the three evils of destiny, which
    were birth, marriage and death, from the Greek
    islands of Chios, Melos, Telos, and Karpathos.

039 Bernard, Harvey R.
    1970. "Paratsoukli": Institutionalized
    Nicknaming in Rural Greece. ETHNOLOGIA
    EUROPAEA 2-3: 65-74.

    Field research was conducted by the author in
    October 1964-November 1965 in the
    sponge-diving island of Kalymnos in order to
    study the social functions of nicknames.
    Nicknaming is widespread in Greece but is
    especially unique in Kalymnos. Nicknames are
    always descriptive of life-cycle events or
    personal characteristics. By studying the
    origin and continuation of the phenomenon, the
    author was able to determine eight distinctive
    features of, names from Kalymnos.

040 Blum, Richard and Eva Blum
    1965. HEALTH AND HEALING IN RURAL GREECE; A
    STUDY OF THREE COMMUNITIES. Stanford: Stanford
    University Press. 269 pp.

    Based on fieldwork done between 1957-1962 to
    study health practices of Greek peasants and
    shepherds, this book studies historical,
    cultural, social, economic, and psychological
    effects on health behavior. Health care from
    antiquity to the present is traced. Folk
    healing, cures, and prevention, as well as
    associated beliefs are examined. The position
    of the folkhealer is studied, including case
    histories with five healers and three healing

priests. A lengthy bibliography on folk
medicine is included.

041 Blum, Richard and Eva Blum
    1970. THE DANGEROUS HOUR: THE LORE OF CRISIS
    AND MYSTERY IN RURAL GREECE. New York:
    Scribner's. 410 pp.

    The Blums' earlier book presented their
    findings on health and healing based on their
    experience living in a central Greek town and
    studying the health and medical practices of
    two villages during the period of 1958-1962.
    This publication presents their observations
    on and examination of the folklore of life and
    death. They gathered many first-hand accounts
    about belief in the supernatural, analyzed the
    narratives from a psychological viewpoint, and
    examined parallels in antiquity.
    Areas covered include beliefs about life-cycle
    events, supernatural creatures and humans
    having supernatural powers, death and the
    dead, exceptional occurrences, afflictions,
    and healing.

042 Bonser, K.J.
    1964. Easter in Greece. FOLKLORE 75: 269-271.

    This brief description of an Athenian Easter
    is based on the author's observations.

043 Bourboulis, Photeine
    1953. STUDIES IN THE HISTORY OF MODERN GREEK
    STORY-MOTIVES. Hellenika Parartema, 2.
    Salonika: s.n. 106 pp.

    This book is actually two essays on the
    migration of folktales: "The Custom of the
    Imperial Bride-Show in Byzantium, its Origin
    and its Creation into a Story-Motif in
    Folk-Literature," studies the picking of a

bride, or bride-show, in history, literature,
and fairy tales in Greece and other countries;
"The Legend of Lucretia and its Survivals in
Modern Greek Folk-Poetry", compares the
original Roman story with other modern and
medieval versions, including a Greek ballad.

044 Bourgault-Ducoudray, Louis-Albert
1876. TRENTE MELODIES POPULAIRES DE GRECE ET
D'ORIENT. Paris: Lemoine. 24, 87 pp.

One of the first collections of text and
music, this book includes thirty songs mainly
from Athens and Smyrna. Greek and Italian text
with French prose renditions.

045 Brewster, Paul G.and Georgia Tarsouli
1945-49. A String Figure Series from Greece.
EPETERIS TOU LAOGRAPHIKOU ARCHEIOU 5: 100-125.

Research on string figures, such as cat's
cradle, is outlined, with specific discussion
of Greek string figures. Nine figures are
shown with description. Forms were collected
in Athens and the south Peloponnesus by
Tarsouli.

046 Brewster, Paul G.
1951. Some Games from Southern Europe. MIDWEST
FOLKLORE 1: 109-111.

This article discusses three games played by
Greek children which were told to the author
by an Athenian in 1948--Kalogeros, Kytsogidi,
and Saliagas. (Three Italian games are also
included.)

047 Brewster, Paul G.
1957. The Legend of Saint Marcella, Virgin
Martyr. WESTERN FOLKLORE 16: 179-183.

Marcella, a virgin, was martyred to protect
herself from becoming a victim of incest.
Miracles came from her transformed martyred
body. This story from the island of Chios is
studied with the text of the story included.

048 Brewster, Paul G. and Georgia Tarsouli.
1961. "HANDJERIS AND LIOYENNETI" AND CHILD 76
AND 110: A STUDY IN SIMILARITIES. FF
Communications 183. Helsinki: Suomalainen
Tiedeakatemia. 17 pp.

In this study, a Greek ballad about a man who
dresses as a woman and seduces a maiden and
his subsequent fate, is compared with two
Child ballads and similar ballads in other
countries. A map shows geographical
distribution of fifty-four Greek texts of the
ballad.

049 Brewster, Paul G.
1977. The Strange Practice of Firewalking.
EXPEDITION 19: 43-47.

In discussing firewalking throughout the
world, Greece is compared with firewalking in
Ceylon, Fiji, India, Spain and Thailand. The
Anastenaria ritual began in 1250 when icons
were saved from a burning church. Firewalking
is performed every year on May 21 as it has
been since 1250.

050 Bürchner, L.
1901-02. Griechische Volksweisen. SAMMELBANDE
DER INTERNATIONALEN MUSIKGESELLSCHAFT 3:
403-429.

This study of folksong texts and music
includes seven songs translated into German.

051 Butler, Francelia
1973. Over the Garden Wall/ I let my Baby
Fall... NEW YORK TIMES MAGAZINE Dec.16, pp.
90-95.

This collection of jump-rope rhymes from five
countries includes one from Greece, as well as
a Greek see-saw rhyme and a picture of Greek
children using an elastic rope.

052 Butterworth, Katharine and Sara Schneider
1975. REBETIKA: SONGS FROM THE OLD GREEK
UNDERWORLD. Athens: Komboloi. 168 pp.

The editors have gathered four essays and
provided text to songs sung and composed
during the first half of the twentieth century
by rebetes, despised people who lived an
underworld existence. Rebetika are songs
about their suffering and dreams.
The essays are: "Rebetika," by Elias
Petropoulos, on the history and development of
rebetika; "The Music of the Rebetes," by
Markos Dragoumis, an historical and
musicological discussion; "The Dances of the
Rebetes," by Ted Petrides; "Rebetika and the
Blues," by Sakis Papdimitriou; "Collection of
Song Lyrics," seventy-four songs translated by
the editors from an anthology by Elias
Petropoulos; and "Musical Examples," the
scores with lyrics for eight songs from
Chapter 5.

053 Campbell, John K.
1964. HONOUR, FAMILY AND PATRONAGE: A STUDY OF
INSTITUTIONS AND MORAL VALUES IN A GREEK
MOUNTAIN COMMUNITY. Oxford: Clarendon Press.
393 pp.

This analysis of social structures of the
Sarakatsani, an ethnic group living in the

northern mountains of Greece, includes
material on religious beliefs and marriage
customs.

054 Caraveli-Chaves, Anna
1980. Bridge Between Worlds: The Greek Women's
Ritual Lament as Communicative Event. JOURNAL
OF AMERICAN FOLKLORE 93: 129-157.

The author studied laments in a Cretan village
that is well-known for its poetry. Laments
are traditionally sung by women. The text of
two variant laments are presented and their
themes examined. Analysis of the texts shows
that lament poetry is full of contrasts, e.g.
mourner/dead, adult/child, individual/world,
past/present, etc. Laments function as
communication with the dead and, therefore,
defeat death. In the process of making
laments the female community is bound
together.

055 Caraveli, Anna
1982. The Song Beyond the Song: Aesthetics and
Social Interaction in Greek Folksong. JOURNAL
OF AMERICAN FOLKLORE 95: 129-158.

By examining what she calls incomplete songs,
Caraveli finds that certain kinds of songs
cannot exist on their own. The world outside
the text, e.g. performer, performance style,
community world view, etc., shapes the meaning
of these songs and these songs are dependent
on that world. She focuses on mantinadhes,
which are couplets, and laments.

056 Carroll, Margaret
1976. IMAGES OF THE AEGEAN: AN ANTHOLOGY OF
MODERN GREEK POETRY. Armidale, Australia:
University of New England Publishing Unit. 125
pp.

The first section of this three-part book is
on folksongs which are presented in four
groups: Historical songs, Love songs, Songs of
everyday life, and Songs of exile and lament.
Titles of the twenty songs are in English with
words in Greek. Songs are summarized,
dialectic features examined, older forms
explained, and historical content provided.

057 Cassidy, Ina Sizer
    1950. Christmas in New Mexico. EL PALACIO 57:
    402-406.

    This article describes Christmas customs of
    Greek miners in New Mexico.

058 Chaves, Anna Caraveli
    1978. LOVE AND LAMENTATION IN GREEK ORAL
    PROSE. Ph.D. dissertation, State University of
    New York, Binghamton. 288 pp. DAI 39/03-A
    p.1531. Order number 78-16656.

    This analysis of style and function of laments
    and love songs determines that these songs are
    not simply expressions of sorrow, but are
    magical songs which join the dead to the
    living.

059 Chianis, Sotirios
    1959. Some Observations on the Mixed-dance in
    the Peloponnesus. LAOGRAPHIA 18: 244-256.

    This article discusses combining dances, a
    common practice in Greece in the 1920s and
    1930s. The author studied mixed-dance type
    songs recorded in various parts of Greece in
    1958-59 to see how dances--in particular,
    Kamatiano and Tsamiko--were mixed.

060 Chianis, Sotirios (Sam)
1965. FOLKSONGS OF MANTINEIA, GREECE. Folklore
Studies, no.15. Berkeley and Los Angeles:
University of California Press. 171 pp.

This collection of sixty-eight village
folksongs from a group of villages in the
province of Mantineia, Arcadia, is published
from a collection of 436 songs collected by
the author in 1958-59, and deposited in the
Folklore and Folk Songs Archives of the
Academy of Athens, and in the archives of the
Insitute of Ethnomusicology, U.C.L.A. Songs
are arranged by type, e.g., Dance songs,
Wedding songs, Laments, etc. For each song
there is the Greek text with musical
transcription, English translation and notes,
and name of singer, village and date
recorded. The introduction includes a
discussion of folk musical instruments.

061 Chianis, Sam (Sotirios)
1966. Aspects of Melodic Ornamentation in the
Folk Music of Cultural Greece. SELECTED
REPORTS, INSTITUTE OF ETHNOMUSICOLOGY 1:
89-119.

An ethnomusicological study on the
significance of complex melodic ornamentation
which is an integral part of Greek folk
music. Melodic ornamentation is part of
peasant and professional folk music for both
instrumentalists and vocalists. Examples are
given.

062 Chianis, Sam (Sotirios)
1967. VOCAL AND INSTRUMENTAL TSAMIKO OF
ROUMELI AND THE PELOPONNESUS. Ph.D.
dissertation, University of California at Los
Angeles. 494 pp. DAI 28/05A p.1835. Order
number 67-14254.
This dissertation analyzes the tsamiko, a type

of folk music and dance from the regions of
Roumeli and the Peloponnesus. The author
collected folk music and analyzed it to
understand the underlying principles, as there
were no real existing studies on this kind of
music. The vocal and instrumental
ornamentation found in tsamiko is examined in
depth.

063 Chourmouziades, A.
     1961. Peri ton Anastenaria kai Allon Tinon
     Parathoxon Ethimon kai Prolepseon [About the
     Anastenaria and Some Other Bizarre Customs and
     Superstitions]. ARCHEION TOU THRAKIKOU
     LAOGRAPHIKOU THESAUROU 26: 143-168. (Original:
     Constantinople, Typos Anatolikou Asteros,
     1873.)

     The first printed source on the Anastenaria,
     this is actually a lecture, requested by the
     Patriarch in Istanbul who needed information
     on the ritual. Based on reports from two
     priests, the Anastenaria is described and said
     to have evolved from Dionysian mysteries. The
     report indicated that persecution strengthened
     the Anastenaria.

064 Christodoulou, Stavroula Potari
     1978. CONTINUITY AND CHANGE AMONG THE
     ANASTENARIA, A FIREWALKING CULT IN NORTHERN
     GREECE. Ph.D. dissertation, State University
     of New York, Stony Brook. 217 pp. DAI 39/10-A
     p.6200. Order number 79-08639.

     The author collected data during the summers
     of 1976 and 1977, and in interviews with
     leaders of the Greek Orthodox Church. This
     dissertation examines the Anastenaria network,
     the firewalking festival itself, including the
     sacrifice, and the function of firewalking and
     related dreaming. History of opposition by
     the Church is included as well as a survey of

Anastenaria: survival of Dionysian mysteries vs. folk religious group. In examining the place of the Anastenaria within the Greek state and within th theoretical framework of religious cults, the author concludes that its members form an ethnic group. Useful glossary and bibliography.

065 Chrysanthis, Kypros
1945. The Personification of Plague and Cholera According to the Cypriots. FOLKLORE 56: 259-266.

Comparison of Greek and Cypriot personifications of these diseases which are usually represented as dirty old women.

066 Chrysanthis, Kyrpos
1946. The Magic Numbers Three, Seven and Seventy-Two in Cypriote Folk-Medicine. FOLKLORE 57: 79-83.

Sacred and magic numbers have been used in curing throughout history in Greece and Cyprus. Popular numbers are discussed here.

067 Codellas, Pan S.
1945. Greek Folklore of the Present Day: the Smerdaki. JOURNAL OF AMERICAN FOLKLORE 58: 236-244.

Description and evolution of the goat-like apparitions, who are similar in appearance to the god Pan and can cause diseases, such as anthrax that destroy entire herds.

068 Constantinides, Elizabeth
1980-81. Folk Ballads of Crete. THE CHARIOTEER 22/23: 130-140.

Two significant collections of the ballads of
Crete were made in the nineteenth century by
Antonios Jeannaraki and in the twentieth
century by Aristides Krias, both Cretans.
Constantinides uses the materials in these
collections as well as her own work in Crete
as the basis for defining the chief
characteristics and subjects of Cretan
ballads.

069 Constantinides, Elizabeth
    1983. Andreiomeni: The Female Warrior in Greek
    Folksongs. JOURNAL OF MODERN GREEK STUDIES 1:
    63-72.

    Although most Greek folksongs show women as
    wives and mothers who are cruel, loving or
    powerless, some ballads have as hero a woman
    who dresses like a man and may fight in
    battle, displays great bravery, be discovered
    in a contest, or die in battle.
    Constantinides examines three ballads, with
    texts in Greek and English, and finds that
    this heroine is a symbol for the never-ending
    battle of the sexes.

070 Coote, H.C.
    1884. Folklore in Modern Greece. FOLKLORE
    JOURNAL 2: 235-243.

    This article summarizes DELTION TES ISTORIKES
    KAI ETHNOLOGIKES ETAIRIAS TES ELLENIKES
    [Transaction of the Historical and
    Ethnological Society of Greece], 1883, which
    included articles on folk medicine and plot
    summaries of folktales.

071 Coulentianou, Joy
    1977. THE GOAT DANCE OF SKYROS. Athens:
    P.Vakalis. 67 pp.

Three weeks before Lent is Apokries, or
Carnival, in Greece. At this time the Gheri,
men dressed in goat hides and many heavy
bells, appear and make a procession through
town. They perform specific dance steps and
play-act with other persons dressed as other
characters. The first part of this book
describes, in both text and pictures, the goat
dance. The second part includes eye-witness
accounts and interpretations from 1835 on, as
well as the author's observations. The
author, who observed the Gheri for more than
fifteen years, interviewed participants and
audience about all aspects of this rite
including origin, which is unknown. She finds
that the procession of the Gheri which used to
be a village psychodrama in which everyone
performed, is now a spectacle for tourists.

072 Crews, Cynthia
    1932. Judaeo-Spanish Folk-tales in Macedonia.
    FOLKLORE 43: 193-225.

    This article includes the text of four lengthy
    tales collected from Balkan Jews in Macedonia
    who speak Ladino. No analysis or comparison.

073 Cutsumbis, Michael N.
    1970. A BIBLIOGRAPHIC GUIDE ON GREEKS IN THE
    UNITED STATES, 1890-1968. New York: Center for
    Migration Studies. 100 pp.

    This bibliography lists books and journal
    articles on Greeks in the United States as
    well as church and fraternal publications,
    unpublished works, doctoral dissertations,
    manuscript collections, and current and
    suspended serials. For works published prior
    to 1953, NATIONAL UNION CATALOG locations are
    given. References to some folklore works are
    provided.

074 Dalven, Rachel
    1973. Betrothal and Marriage Customs of the
    Jannina Jews. SEPHARDIC SCHOLAR 3:41-60.

    The Jewish community of Ioannina before World
    War II was large, prosperous, and old.
    Dalven, a descendant of Ioannina Jews,
    describes the stages of courtship and marriage
    of Greek Jews of Ioannina in detail. Sources
    are her parents, relatives, and friends from
    Ioannina.

075 Dalven, Rachel
    1974. The Yearly Cycle of the Ioannina Jews.
    CONSERVATIVE JUDAISM 2:47-53.

    Dalven describes in detail the customs
    practices, and foods of the Sabbath and
    holidays of Greek Jews in pre-World War II
    Ioannia.

076 Danforth, Loring M.
    1976. Humour and Status Reversal in Greek
    Shadow Theatre. BYZANTINE AND MODERN GREEK
    STUDIES 2: 99-111.

    This examination of humor and transformation
    or reversal of social relationships focuses on
    traditional Greek shadow plays. Danforth
    discusses the relationships between the
    central character, Karaghiozis, and the stock
    characters, and studies their joking/insulting
    interactions and Karaghiozis' blurring of
    social boundaries. This status reversal
    affects the audience and makes them identify
    strongly with their culture.

077 Danforth, Loring M.
    1978. THE ANASTENARIA: A STUDY IN GREEK RITUAL
    THERAPY. Ph.D. dissertation, Princeton

University. 412 pp. DAI 39/04-A p.2382.
Order number 78-18324.

The Anastenaria is a ritual involving trance,
possession, and firewalking. The social
organization of the Anastenarides and the
symbolic function of ritual are analyzed in
Danforth's dissertation, based on fourteen
months of fieldwork in Greek Macedonia in
1975-76. He describes in detail the
Anastenaria, before 1914 and in 1976, as well
as the diagnostic and healing powers of the
performers.

078 Danforth, Loring M.
     1979. The Role of the Dance in the Ritual
     Therapy of the Anastenaria. BYZANTINE AND
     MODERN GREEK STUDIES 5: 141-163.

The role of the dance performed by the
Anastenarides is seen as therapeutic in that
it offers a cathartic release of emotions
which may have been responsible for illness.
The dancers are in a trance and walk barefoot
on hot coals. Persons who are cured by
participating in the dance often become
official Anastenarides. This article is based
on Danforth's fieldwork in Greek Macedonia in
1975-76 and includes accounts of the dance's
therapeutic effects on some specific
individuals.

079 Danforth, Loring
     1982. THE DEATH RITUALS OF RURAL GREECE.
     Photography by Alexander Tsiaras. Princeton:
     Princeton University Press. 169 pp.

In 1975-76 Tsiaras made a photographic study
of the rituals that relate to death in a
village in northern Greece. In 1979, on
Tsiaras' suggestion, Danforth did fieldwork in
that same village on death rituals of rural

Greece. The first part of the book is
Danforth's description and analysis of the
death rites, including the text of many
laments. The second section is Tsiaras'
photographic essay with descriptive text
accompanying each plate.

080 Danforth, Loring M.
1983. Power Through Submission in the
Anastenaria. JOURNAL OF MODERN GREEK STUDIES
1: 203-223.

The first part of this article is an
examination of women's power in rural Greece.
The author suggests that the existing notions
of public and private spheres of social
interaction be modified based on his fieldwork
in Greek Macedonia in 1975-76. The second part
is an analysis of women's role in the
Anastenaria, the ritual celebration of
St.Constantine, in which female participants,
called Anastenarides, are possessed by the
saint. Danforth finds that these women gain
status and power in the community only by
submitting to the male cult leaders, the
spirit of the male saint, and the wills of
their husbands. Interviews with village women
are included.

081 Danforth, Loring M.
1983. Tradition and Change in Greek Shadow
Theater. JOURNAL OF AMERICAN FOLKLORE 96:
281-309.

Greek shadow theater was very popular at the
end of the nineteenth and beginning of the
twentieth centuries, but was eventually
overshadowed by mass entertainment. Interest
in shadow theater waxed in the 1970s when
comic books appeared starring Karaghiozis as a
contemporary character such as James Bond or
an astronaut. In this article Danforth

compares the current plays with the more traditional ones by examining their plots according to Propp's theory of syntagmatic structural analysis. He shows that Greek shadow theater is a dynamic narrative tradition that, nevertheless, maintains its tradition.

082 Danforth, Loring M.
1984. The Ideological Context of the Search for Continuities in Greek Culture. JOURNAL OF MODERN GREEK STUDIES 2: 53-85.

The author of this article contends that the study of folklore, religion and ritual of modern Greek rural culture has mainly looked for survivals and, therefore, treats the modern culture as "fossilized relics of ancient Greek culture" (p.53). Harmful effects of this approach include negating the importance of the modern community, creating distance between subject and scholar, and not seeing the modern culture as a valid whole. Because the academic study of Greek folklore study developed with political goals of establishing a link between ancient and modern Greece, continuity of culture was emphasized more than comparisons with other cultures.

083 Dawkins, Richard M.
1904-1905. A Visit to Skyros: the Carnival. ANNUAL OF THE BRITISH SCHOOL OF ATHENS. 11: 72-74.

In March 1905, the author was on Skyros and present at the Carnival. In this short article he describes the play and its characters, as well as the ritual dance performed by shepherds dressed in goat hides and many goat bells, called the Gheri.

084 Dawkins, Richard M.
     1906. The Modern Carnival in Thrace and the
     Cult of Dionysus. JOURNAL OF HELLENIC STUDIES
     26: 191-206.

     This description of a village festival in 1906
     includes discussion of its relationship to the
     ancient festivals of Dionysus and detailed
     descriptions of costumes worn and characters
     portrayed.

085 Dawkins, Richard M.
     1916. MODERN GREEK IN ASIA MINOR: A STUDY OF
     THE DIALECTS OF SILLI, CAPPADOCIA AND PHARASA.
     Cambridge: University Press, 695 pp.

     This study on the modern Greek dialects of
     Asia Minor includes ninety-five folktales
     dictated or written by villagers where Dawkins
     did his research. Included is a chapter on
     the subjects of the tales, plus a
     bibliography, by W.R.Halliday.

086 Dawkins, Richard M.
     1923. "The Twelve Months": A Folktale from
     Pontus. LAOGRAPHIA 7: 285-291.

     Text and translation of a folktale from Imera,
     Pontus collected by Dawkins in 1914.

087 Dawkins, Richard M.
     1930. Folk-memory in Crete. FOLKLORE 61:
     11-42.

     In this 1930 Presidential address to the
     Folklore Society, Dawkins outlines the history
     of Crete as shown in ballads, stories,
     customs, sayings and religious practices.

088 Dawkins, R.M.

1931. Folktales from the Surmena and the
Valley of Ophis. ARCHEION PONTOU [Archives of
Pontus] 3: 79-122.

This article includes the text of twenty-three
tales in Greek collected in interviews from
boys and men in 1914 in Surmena and Ophis.
Linguistic notes with each tale.

089 Dawkins, Richard M.
1934. Some Modern Greek Songs from Cappadocia.
AMERICAN JOURNAL OF ARCHAEOLOGY 38: 112-122.

An examination of four songs from the Levidis
manuscript collection of late nineteenth
century folklore and linguistic material.
Three songs have Digenis Akritas as the
subject and the fourth concerns a bridge built
by Charon to the underworld. The texts of the
songs are in Greek and English.

090 Dawkins, Richard M.
1942. Folklore in Stories from the Dodecanese.
FOLKLORE 53: 5-26.

This state of the art essay on Greek folklore,
in particular storytelling, discusses the
first collections of Greek folktales by
Zarraftis, Rouse, Adamantiou, and Pio,
includes stories and discusses some of their
themes.

091 Dawkins, R.M.
1942. Modern Greek Oral Versions of
Appollonius of Trye. MODERN LANGUAGE REVIEW
37: 169-184.

In studying versions of an oral story by
Appollonius of Trye, Dawkins explains why the
story changed over time to suit new audiences,
with new themes and motifs added. Versions

from Kos, collected by Joseph Zarraftis, are
compared to other Greek versions. Translation
of one version is included.

092 Dawkins, Richard M.
    1942. Soul and Body in the Folklore of Modern
    Greece. FOLKLORE 53: 131-147.

    A lecture on Christian and primitive beliefs
    concerning the fate of the soul after death,
    this article carefully examines the idea of
    Charos and his role in death as expressed in
    dirges, songs, and folktales.

093 Dawkins, Richard M.
    1942-43. The Art of Story-Telling in the
    Dodekanese. BYZANTION: INTERNATIONAL JOURNAL
    OF BYZANTINE STUDIES, American Series II 16:
    357-380.

    This discussion of storytelling is based on a
    manuscript of Joseph Zarraftis of Kos, who
    collected folktales for W.H.D.Rouse in the
    early twentieth century (circa 1904). A few of
    the stories were fairy stories but most were
    original. Unfortunately, Zarraftis provided
    no information about the storyteller or
    audience. Dawkins discusses discerning who is
    narrator of a story and finds that most of
    these stories show the world the way it was
    for the Greek peasant of the time. The texts
    of some stories are included.

094 Dawkins, Richard M.
    1944. "The Schoolmaster and the Holy Elder," a
    Modern Greek Folktale. FOLKLORE 55: 150-161.

    Dawkins relates and studies the folktale "The
    School Master and the Holy Elder" from the
    Rouse/Zarraftis collection of folktales.

095 Dawkins, Richard M.
     1948. Some Remarks on Greek Folk-tales.
     FOLKLORE 59: 49-68.

     In this article the author recounts and
     discusses many moral stories and fairy tales
     from the Rouse/Zarraftis collection as well as
     stories he collected himself, and examines how
     they change with travel and time, take on
     local characteristics, and adapt local
     customs. Elements from some of these tales
     can be traced to classical stories.

096 Dawkins, Richard M.
     1950. FORTY-FIVE STORIES FROM THE DODECANESE.
     Cambridge: Cambridge University Press. 560 pp.

     This book provides texts of stories with
     English translations from the Zarraftis
     manuscript collection of tales from Kos and
     three other Dodecanese islands. No
     information about informants was provided by
     Zarraftis. Included are lengthy notes on each
     story and an introduction to storytelling in
     the Dodecanese.

097 Dawkins, Richard M.
     1951. Recently Published Collections of Modern
     Folktales. ANNUAL OF THE BRITISH SCHOOL AT
     ATHENS 46: 53-60.

     This article surveys published books of
     folktales in many languages, including Greek
     folktales.

098 Dawkins, Richard M.
     1952. "The Silent Princess." FOLKLORE 63:
     129-142.

     This articles relates and discusses stories

which have as the main theme the silence of a
woman, usually a princess.

099 Dawkins, Richard M.
1953. In a Greek Village. FOLKLORE 64:
386-396.

This article on dancing, singing, and
storytelling activity includes description of
some dances and ballads.

100 Dawkins, Richard M.
1953. MODERN GREEK FOLKTALES. Oxford:
Clarendon Press. 491 pp.

Eighty-three stories collected from
manuscripts, books and journal articles, with
introductions and Aarne-Thompson type numbers
are presented here. Locations of variant
texts are given.

101 Dawkins, Richard M.
1953. "The Two Bets," A Reconstructed Greek
Folktale. LAOGRAPHIA 15: 147-150.

Five stories are related here which have as
the main subject a hero's two bets: 1) lose
all his property, 2) regain it.

102 Dawkins, Richard M.
1955. The Boy's Dream. MIKRASIATIKA CHRONIKA
[Asia Minor Chronicle] 6: 268-282.

Dawkins took this folktale from the
manuscripts of Anastasios Levidis, a scholar
and teacher who collected linguistic material,
songs, proverbs, and myths in Cappadocia in
the late nineteenth century. The study of
"the boy's dream," which is found in eastern
Europe and Greece, outlines the study in

English. The Greek text is known as "The Son
of the Villager."

103 Dawkins, Richard M.
1955. MORE GREEK TALES. Oxford: Clarendon
Press. 178 pp.

This collection presents twenty-six stories
not published in Dawkins' MODERN GREEK
FOLKTALES (1953). For each folktale there is
an introduction and discussion.

104 Dawkins, Richard M.
1956-57. The Man who Went out to Seek Fear. In
MELANGES OFFERTS A OCTAVE ET MELPO MERLIER A
L'OCCASION DU 25E ANNIVERSAIRE DE LEUR ARRIVEE
EN GRECE, vol.1. pp.181-187. Athens:
L'Institut Francais d'Athènes.

In this article Dawkins examines the few Greek
versions of a tale frequently found in other
parts of Europe and compares it to those from
other countries.

105 Deter-Grohmann, Ismene
1968. DAS NEUGRIECHISCHE VOLKSLIED.
DARGESTELLT AM BEISPIEL AUSGEWAHLTER
GATTUNGEN. Munich: Ernst Heimeran. 99 pp.

This book serves as a good introduction to the
rich folksong tradition of Greece. Features of
the folksong and major varieties of folksongs
are discussed. Songs are translated into
German.

106 Deligiorgis, Stavros
1969. Fauriel and Modern Greek Poetry.
PROCEEDINGS OF THE MODERN LANGUAGE ASSOCIATION
84: 9-13.

This article reviews the criticism of Claude
Fauriel's collection of Greek folksongs
(1824-25). The major points for criticism have
been including folksongs with non-folksongs
and Fauriel's romanticism.

107 Dieterich, Karl
1902. Die Volksdichtung der Balkanländer in
ihren gemeinsamen Elementen. ZEITSCHRIFT DES
VEREINS FUR VOLKSUNDE 12: 145-155, 272-291,
403-415.

This article compares and analyzes Rumanian,
Albanian, and Slavic folksongs with Greek
folksong.

108 Dimaras, C.Th., C.Koumarianou, and L.Droulia
1968. MODERN GREEK CULTURE: A SELECTED
BIBLIOGRAPHY. Thessaloniki: Institute for
Balkan Studies. 137 pp.

Section 16, Medieval and Folk Literature,
Collections, lists books that are collections
of songs, tales, poems, proverbs, and
sayings. Tables of contents of BALKAN
STUDIES, 1960-68, vols.1-9, are included.

109 Dionisopoulos-Mass, Regina
1976. The Evil Eye and Bewitchment in a
Peasant Village. In THE EVIL EYE, ed.Clarence
Maloney. pp.42-62. New York: Columbia
University Press.

This article examines the dynamic relationship
between the evil eye, gossip, and magic, as
well as protective measures used on people,
animals and inanimate objects. Based on
fieldwork on the demography and ethnology of a
Greek island village in 1970 and 1971-72.

110 Doering, Eileen Elita
   1939. A Charm of the Gulf of Mexico Sponge
   Fishers. JOURNAL OF AMERICAN FOLKLORE 52: 123.

   A single paragraph description of a charm used
   by Greek sponge divers working in the Gulf of
   Mexico.

111 Doering, J. Frederick
   1943. Folk Customs and Beliefs of Greek Sponge
   Fishers in Florida. SOUTHERN FOLKLORE
   QUARTERLY 7: 105-107.

   A description of various customs: charms for
   good weather and for finding sponges,and
   practices surrounding the festival of
   Epiphany, including retrieving the cross from
   the water.

112 Dorson, Richard
   1957. Tales of a Greek-American Family on
   Tape. FABULA 1: 114-143. and errata FABULA 2:
   202-203, 1958.

   Interviews with a family from Bambakou,
   Greece, living in Iron City, Michigan, include
   personal narratives of immigration and
   accounts of adventures of relatives in World
   War I and wars with the Turks in the early
   19th century. Most of the narratives deal
   with their home town and the beliefs and
   stories associated with it.

113 Dorson, Richard
   1959. Immigrant Folklore. In AMERICAN
   FOLKLORE, Richard Dorson. pp.135-165.
   Chicago: University of Chicago Press.

   A section of this chapter describes Dorson's
   fieldwork with a Greek immigrant family in
   Michigan in 1955. [see entry above]

114 du Boulay, Juliet
    1974. PORTRAIT OF A GREEK MOUNTAIN VILLAGE.
    Oxford: Clarendon Press. 296 pp.

    Based on fieldwork done between 1966-68, this
    ethnography of a Euboean village includes data
    on belief, marriage, customs, and religious
    rituals.

115 du Boulay, Juliet
    1982. The Greek Vampire: A Study of Cyclic
    Symbolism in Marriage and Death. MAN 17:
    219-239.

    Based on fieldwork conducted in 1971-73, in a
    village in northern Euboea, this article
    analyzes the role of blood in funeral and
    marriage rites. Death and burial are
    described with emphasis on how one is proved
    to be a vampire.

116 Dulakis, Carrie C.
    1982. FREEDOM PLAYS THE FLUTE: A SELECTION
    FROM THE FOLK POETRY OF MODERN GREECE.
    Smithtown, NY: Exposition. 119 pp.

    This book is the English translation of more
    than sixty folksongs which the author has
    taken from printed sources published between
    1825 and 1940. It includes songs of the
    islands, klephtic songs, Akritan songs, round
    dances, carols and popular songs. Explanatory
    notes accompany some songs.

117 Duran, Lucy
    1975. Greek Folk Music: A Selective and
    Annotated Discography. MANDATOPHOROS 6: 9-23.

    Attempts to given "an accurate picture of

Greek folk music as it is performed today."

118 Edmonds, E.M.
    1884. Notes on Greek Folklore. FOLKLORE
    JOURNAL 2: 168-172.

    This article describes burial customs, evil
    eye beliefs and superstitions from Crete and
    Cyrpus as observed by the author.

119 Evelpidis, Christos
    1964. Anastenaria, une culte, dionysiaque
    contemporain. CAHIERS DU SUD 51, no.377:
    [i-v] in Lettre de Macedonie.

    This article describes the ritual of the
    Anastenaria in the village of Langadas.
    Theories of origin are examined, particularly
    possible evolution from mysteries in honor of
    Dionysus to rites for Sts.Constantine and
    Helen.

120 Fauriel, Claude
    1824-25. CHANTS POPULAIRES DE LA GRECE
    MODERNE. Paris: Didot. 2 vols. 144, 303 pp.,
    499 pp.

    This first major collection of Greek demotic
    folksongs includes klephtic, historical,
    romantic, domestic and wedding songs. In the
    introduction Fauriel states his support of the
    theory that modern folk poetry can be directly
    traced to the poetry of antiquity.

121 Fermor, Patrick Leigh
    1958. MANI: TRAVELS IN THE SOUTHERN
    PELOPONNESE. New York: Harper and Row. 320 pp.

    This travelogue describes in detail the Maniat
    way of life, including history, legends and

folklore.

122 Fermor, Patrick Leigh
1962. ROUMELI: TRAVELS IN NORTHERN GREECE. New
York: Harper and Row. 248 pp.

Roumeli is the region between Macedonia and
the Gulfs of Corinth and Salamis, and is the
home of the sheepherding tribe, the
Sarakatsani. This travel account describes
their way of life, including festivals,
beliefs, and marriage and funeral customs.

123 Frazer, James George
1890. Easter in Greece. FOLKLORE 1: 275-276.

This article describes Easter in Athens as
observed by the author in 1890. Easter rituals
in various parts of Greece are discussed.

124 Frazer, James George
1890. May Day in Greece. FOLKLORE 1: 518-520.

This account of May Day customs in 1889 from
various parts of Greece includes the
translated text of a song sung in Corfu.

125 Frye, Ellen
1973. THE MARBLE THRESHING FLOOR: A COLLECTION
OF GREEK FOLKSONGS. Austin: University of
Texas Press. American Folklore Society, Memoir
Series, vol.57. 326 pp.

The author recorded songs during trips to
Greece in 1963-64 and 1967, most of which were
unknown to the Folklore Archives of the
Academy of Athens. 110 songs are arranged by
region with text, musical transcription,
translation of lyrics, name of singer and
place recorded, and notes for each song.

Notes usually include function or context of song. An index of Greek titles and first lines is included.

126 Garnett, Lucy Mary Jane
    1885. GREEK FOLK-SONGS FROM THE TURKISH PROVINCES OF GREECE...LITERAL AND METRICAL TRANSLATIONS. London: E. Stock. 260 pp.

    A collection of 155 songs from Albania, Thessaly, and Macedonia from published collections of Greek songs and translated by Garnett. Major subject areas are Mythological, Affectional (Erotic, Domestic and Humouristic), and Historical folksongs. This work includes an essay by J.S.Stuart-Glennie, "The Survival of Paganism."

127 Garnett, Lucy Mary Jane
    1888. GREEK FOLKSONGS FROM THE OTTOMAN PROVINCES OF NORTHERN HELLAS. London: Ward and Downey. 288 pp.

    For this book the author translated and classified more than 150 songs from Albania, Thessaly, and Macedonia, taken from published collections. Major subject areas are Mythological, Affectional (Erotic, Domestic and Humouristic), and Historical.

128 Garnett, Lucy M.J.
    1892. The Widow's Son. FOLKLORE 3: 265-266.

    This article cites six folktales and songs in published works that show a widow's son as a hero.

129 Garnett, Lucy M.J. and J.S.Stuart-Glennie
    1896. GREEK FOLK POESY. ANNOTATED TRANSLATIONS FROM THE WHOLE CYCLE OF ROMAIC FOLK-VERSE AND FOLK-PROSE. London: Nutt. 2 vols. 477 pp.,

541 pp.

Volume 1 is on folksongs and includes
mythological, social, and historical
folksongs, and an essay on Greek folk speech.
Volume 2, on the folktale, includes
mythological folktales, social folk-stories,
historical folk legends and an essay on the
survival of paganism. All poetry, songs,
ballads, tales and legends, etc., are
translated from printed sources. Also
included are essays entitled "The Science of
Folklore," "Greek Folk Speech," and "The
Survival of Paganism."

130 Garnett, Lucy Mary Jane
    1917. BALKAN HOME-LIFE. New York: Dodd, Mead.
    309 pp.

    Chapters 5, 6, and 7 are on Greeks, including
    one on ceremonies and one on beliefs and
    superstitions.

131 Gauntlett, Stathis
    1982-83. Rebetiko Tragoudi as a Generic Term.
    BYZANTINE AND MODERN GREEK STUDIES, 8: 77-102.

    This article surveys the problems and disputes
    in rebetiko scholarship, in particular: social
    context, origin and demise, and folkloric
    status; and the problems of definition.
    Development and change in song themes from
    mid-nineteenth century to post-World War II,
    as rebetiko became popular and commercial, is
    examined. The author argues that the emphasis
    on using a generic term for a type of song
    should be on describing the body of songs, and
    that more scholarly work on rebetiko music
    needs to be done.

132 Geldart, Edward M.

1884. THE FOLKLORE OF MODERN GREECE. THE TALES
OF THE PEOPLE... London: Sonnenschein. 190 pp.

Twenty-nine tales translated from printed
sources. (Twenty-six are from Pio.)

133 Georgeakis, G., and Leon Pineau
1894. LE FOLKLORE DE LESBOS. Paris:
Maisonneuve. 349 pp.

Collected folklore of Lesbos including
folktales, songs, proverbs, and superstitions.

134 Georges, Robert A.
1962. Greek Folk Remedy in America. SOUTHERN
FOLKLORE QUARTERLY 26: 122-126.

The venduza is a folk remedy which can cure
colds, pneumonia, and back ache. It is
performed by putting glasses over flames and
then on the ailing part of a person's body.
The author interviewed Greek-Americans about
the venduza and found many variations.

135 Georges, Robert A.
1962. Matiasma: Living Folk Belief. MIDWEST
FOLKLORE 3: 69-74.

The principal cause of the evil eye is
excessive praise or admiration. This article
discusses how matiasma is caused and
protective measures taken against it.

136 Georges, Robert A.
1964. GREEK-AMERICAN FOLK BELIEFS AND
NARRATIVES: SURVIVALS AND LIVING TRADITION.
Ph.D. dissertation, Indiana University. 251
pp. 26/09 p.5360. Order number 64-12023.

The author collected material on the

supernatural from Tarpon Springs, Savannah,
Wichita Falls, Texas, Cincinnati, and New York
City, by interviewing Greek-Americans. He
found that many superstitions crossed the
ocean but, for the most part, belief in demons
and spirits remained in Greece. Such beliefs
are significant in that they validate
religious practices, reinforce belief in
magic, and perpetuate ethnic and cultural
values.

137 Georges, Robert A.
1965. The Greeks of Tarpon Springs: An
American Folk Group. SOUTHERN FOLKLORE
QUARTERLY 24: 129-141.

Based on extensive fieldwork during the
summers of 1961 and 1962, the author studied
many magico-religious beliefs amd concluded
that the most persistent beliefs are those
which are closely bound up with the homeland
religion but not sanctioned by the Greek
Orthodox Church.

138 Georges, Robert A.
1978. Conceptions of Fate in Stories told by
Greeks. In FOLKLORE IN THE MODERN WORLD,
ed.Richard M. Dorson. pp.301-319. The Hague:
Mouton.

This article discusses conceptions of fate or
destiny which are usually found in the forms
of the Fates, Lady Luck, or God, as expressed
by Greek storytellers. Five stories are given
as examples.

139 Georges, Robert A.
1979. Feedback and Response in Storytelling.
WESTERN FOLKLORE 38: 104-110.

The storyteller's response to his own material

is important and is an aspect often overlooked by folklorists. Georges uses a performance of a Greek-American from Kalymnos and a story he told in 1964 as an example.

140 Giagannos, Ap., Ar.Giagannos, and I.Dinkles
1976. O KOΣMOΣ TOU KAΡAGHIOZIΣ: FIGOURES [The World of Karaghiozis: Figures]. Athens: Ermis. 240 pp.

This book is an illustrated guide to the stock characters of the Karaghiozis shadow theater.

141 Gizelis, Gregory
1970. Foodways Acculturation in the Greek Community of Philadelphia. PENNSYLVANIA FOLKLIFE 20(1): 9-15.

For this study of the changes Greek food has undergone in America, the author interviewed Greek-Americans about food preparation, substitutions, cooking, storing and freezing.

142 Gizelis, Gregory
1971. The Use of Amulets among Greek Philadelphians. PENNSYLVANIA FOLKLIFE 20(3): 30-37.

This article describes different types of amulets, studies their sources and functions, and briefly discusses the history of amulet wearing by Greeks. Interviews indicate that wearers of amulets believe they can prevent danger, violence, and ill health, and save lives. Photographs of amulets are included.

143 Gizelis, Gregory
1972. Historical Event into Song: The Use of Cultural Perceptual Style. FOLKLORE 83: 302-320.

The first part of this article is a discussion
of the various theories as to how historical
events are made into songs. The second
section examines Greek historical folksongs
from the 17th, 18th and 19th centuries.
Gizelis finds that people have
culturally-bound perceptual styles which
affect the way they express their experiences.

144 Gizelis, Gregory
    1973. Greek Traditional Medical Practices as
    Revealed in a Manuscript from the Island of
    Levkas. KEYSTONE FOLKLORE 18: 103-126.

    Texts, contextual data, and analysis for
    exorcisms, cures, charms, and healing
    processes as found in a late-19th century
    manuscript. The owners of the manuscript
    believed it to have curative powers.

145 Gizelis, Gregory
    1973. A Neglected Aspect of Creativity of
    Folklore Performers. JOURNAL OF AMERICAN
    FOLKLORE 86: 167-172.

    The author believes that real creativity in
    folklore performances has not been studied as
    much or as seriously as re-creation and
    limited creation. This article presents three
    stories of original creation from 1970-71
    fieldwork with Greek-Americans in
    Philadelphia.

146 Gizelis, Gregory
    1974. The Function of the Vision in
    Greek-American Culture. WESTERN FOLKLORE 33:
    66-76.

    This examination of religious revelations
    which are usually associated with icons and

sacred objects, and are mainly experienced by
women, includes six interviews with
visionaries of the Philadelphia Greek-American
community. The author finds that religious
visions are a cultural phenomenon, not private
and accidental.

147 Gizelis, Gregory
    1974. NARRATIVE RHETORICAL DEVICES OF
    PERSUASION: FOLKLORE COMMUNICATION IN A
    GREEK-AMERICAN COMMUNITY. Athens: National
    Centre of Social Research. 155 pp.

    Based on author's 1972 dissertation, this
    discussion of storytelling among
    Greek-Americans in Philadelphia focuses on the
    relationship between narrative and group
    self-definition, in particular the effect of
    story-telling on attitude and value
    formation. Texts of more than forty jokes,
    puns and stories are included as they were
    tape-recorded.

148 Gizelis, Gregory
    1980. NARRATIVE RHETORICAL DEVICES OF
    PERSUASION IN THE GREEK COMMUNITY OF
    PHILADELPHIA. New York: Arno. 264 pp.
    (Original: Ph.D. dissertation, University of
    Pennsylvania, 1972.)

    Based on fieldwork with Greek-Americans in
    Philadelphia between 1970-71, this
    dissertation examines the ways in which
    folklore is involved in the formation of
    beliefs, attitudes, behavior and values as
    displayed in storytelling. The texts of tales
    as they were recorded are included. The
    introductory chapter is an essay on
    Greek-American folklore scholarship.

149 Glaser, Richard

1976. Greek Jews in Baltimore. JEWISH SOCIAL
STUDIES 38: 321-336.

This article compares the Greek Jews of Athens
and Salonika and describes their immigration
to the United States, in particular, to
Baltimore. The discussion of changes in
religious observances, holiday customs,
cooking, naming and birth practices, and
superstitious beliefs is based on the author's
survey of twenty-eight Greek Jews living in
Baltimore.

150 Gravel, Pierre Bettez
1978. A Legend in the Making: Manolas, the
Pirate. JOURNAL OF THE FOLKLORE INSTITUTE 15:
253-262.

A saga from the island of Kynthos about
Manolas, the bandit, who lived in the
nineteenth and twentieth centuries, based on
fieldwork done in 1971-72. The narratives
included are from local people, including
members of Manolas' family.

151 Gregoire, Henri
1942. DIGENIS AKRITAS, THE BYZANTINE EPIC IN
HISTORY AND POETRY. NY: National Herald. 336
pp.

Written in Greek to encourage scholars to
learn the language, this book studies the
Byzantine Digenis epic and popular ballads.
Gregoire examines their place in history,
compares them to other epics and ballads, and
outlines the various editions and
translations. He contends that the epic came
from the folksongs and was preserved not by
manuscripts but by oral tradition.

152 Grinsell, Leslie Valentine

1957. The Ferryman and his fee: A study in
Ethnology, Archaeology and Tradition. FOLKLORE
68: 257-269.

This article mainly deals with Charon in
antiquity but section 6 briefly discusses
contemporary practice of burying coins with
the dead in Macedonia, Thrace, and Asia Minor.

153 Gubbins, J.K.
1946-47. Some Observations on the Evil Eye in
Modern Greece. FOLKLORE 57: 195-198.

Observations on belief in the evil eye as held
by educated persons, including methods of
curing and preventing the evil eye.

154 Hadjicosta, Ismene
1943. CYPRUS AND ITS LIFE, MORALS AND CUSTOMS
OF CYPRUS FOLKSONGS,-ETC. Translated by
D.A.Percival. London: s.n. English, 48 pp.
Greek, 93 pp.

Much of the material presented here was
gathered by the author from Greek-Cypriots
living in London. The first section covers
history and the second is on folklore,
including marriage, funerals, harvest customs,
calendar festivals, charms (five, with text
and description), and a Cypriot folktale. Not
a scholarly work but done by an ex-patriot who
wanted to preserve these traditions in
writing.

155 Hadjicosta, Ismene
1944. Some Traditional Customs of the People
of Cyprus. FOLKLORE 55/56: 107-117.

Detailed descriptions of marriage, burial, and
holiday customs of Cypriots.

156 Hadjimihali, Angheliki
1937. L'ART POPULAIRE GREC. Athens: Pyrsos.
160 pp. (Original: Hellenike Laike Techne.
Athens, 1925.)

This important book describes the popular art
movement that revived folk arts. Hadjimihali
was indefatiguably dedicated to preserving and
recording traditional life. In this book she
describes, in individual chapters and with
photographs, architecture, painting, applied
arts, costume, weaving, embroidery, lace work,
wood work, ceramics, metal work, and
smithing. Formation of craft associations,
support for folk arts and their significance
in tourism, and the role of folk art museums
are covered. A lengthy bibliography on Greek
popular art is included.

157 Hadjimihali, Angheliki
1949. LA MAISON GRECQUE. Athens: L'Hellenisme
Contemporain. 44 pp.

This book on popular architecture describes in
detail two principal types of Greek houses:
the Mediterranean or Aegean house, and the
Middle-Class house. Exteriors and interiors
are described with some discussion of
furniture, use of rooms and use of space. It
is illustrated with drawings, photographs and
floor plans.

158 Hadjimihali, Angheliki
1950. LA SCULPTURE SUR BOIS. Athens:
L'Hellenisme Contemporain. 58 pp.

There are two categories of wood sculpture: 1)
geometric abstract and symbolism, and 2) urban
and religious art. A history of wood scupture
is provided but there is little information on

the artisans themselves. Photographs of wood
sculptures and drawings illustrate this
booklet.

159 Hadjimihali, Angheliki
1951. La Semaine Sainte et Paques chez les
Saracatsans. L'HELLENISME CONTEMPORAIN, ser.2,
année 5: 131-136.

This article describes Holy Week and Easter as
observed by the Sarakatsan tribe.

160 Hadjimihali, Angheliki
1969. Greek Regional Costumes. CIBA REVIEW 2:
35-44.

This article discusses the development of
Greek regional costume, including festival,
everyday, and court dress.

161 Hadjimihali, Angheliki
1977. GREEK FOLK COSTUME: COSTUMES WITH THE
SIGOUNI, text researcher and compiler Tataiana
Ioannou-Yiannara. Athens: Melissa. 339 pp.

This is the first part of Angheliki
Hadjimihali's great work on Greek national
costume which was turned over to the Benaki
Museum after her death in 1965. The
introduction by Ioannou-Yiannara is a brief
discussion on Greek costume study. Costumes
which use the white woolen coat, called the
sigouni, are described by region in eighteen
chapters with accompanying drawings and
photographs of costumes from the Benaki
Museum.

162 Hadjioannou, Kyriakos
1965 Four Types of External Soul in Greek and
other Folk-Narratives. LAOGRAPHIA 22: 140-150.

The external soul signifies the belief that a
being's soul can be parted from the body and
hidden so that its owner cannot be
destroyed. This motif appears in numerous
Greek folk narratives. In this article the
tales are classified into four types.

163 Hahn, Johann Georg von
   1864. GRIECHISCHE UND ALBANESICHE MARCHEN.
   Leipzig: Engelmann. 2 vols. 319 pp., 339 pp.

   Volume 1 contains sixty-one Greek folktales
   translated into German with copious notes.
   Tales were either collected by the author or
   for him. Arrangement is by region.

164 Halliday, W.R.
   1912. Folklore Scraps from Greece and Asia
   Minor. FOLKLORE 23: 218-220.

   This article is a collection of miscellaneous
   beliefs and customs as observed by the author
   in 1911, many in Cappadocia.

165 Halliday, W.R.
   1912. A Greek Marriage in Cappadocia. FOLKLORE
   23: 81-88.

   This article describes a wedding in a large
   Cappadocian village as observed by the
   author. The pre-wedding ritual, the ceremony
   and taboos were explained to him in detail.
   Includes four photographs.

166 Halliday, W.R.
   1912-1914. Modern Greek Folk-Tales and Ancient
   Greek Mythology. FOLKLORE 23: 486-487/25:
   122-125.

These articles challenge the idea that a
specific tale concerning Demeter is a survival
from antiquity. An ancient and a modern story
are compared.

167 Halliday, W.R.
1913. Cretan Folklore Notes. FOLKLORE 24:
357-359.

A collection of miscellaneous beliefs and
customs from Crete, this article includes a
description and photograph of binding a
church. When a village is devastated by an
epidemic, the exterior of the church is tied
with candles.

168 Hamilton, Mary
1910. GREEK SAINTS AND THEIR FESTIVALS.
Edinburgh: William Blackwood. 211 pp.

Based on research in Greece and Italy in
1907-1909, a study of functions and names of
saints, their festivals and related customs
and rituals. Hamilton presents contemporary
beliefs and practices as well as examining
survivals from antiquity.

169 Hardie, Margaret M. (Mrs. F.W.Hasluck)
1923. The Evil Eye in Some Greek Villages of
the Upper Haliakmon Valley in West Macedonia.
JOURNAL OF THE ROYAL ANTHROPOLOGICAL INSTITUTE
OF GREAT BRITAIN AND IRELAND. 53: 160-172.

This article is on the nature of remedies for
the evil eye, including cases of persons
afflicted with the evil eye, methods of
prevention, and remedies. The author managed
to get the texts of eight complex charms, a
difficult task since they are not to be
transferred by voice. Hardie tells how she
persuaded people to talk to her about the evil

eye and states that the charms were given to
her in writing. In analyzing the charms she
found recurring motifs.

170 Hardie, Margaret M. (Mrs. F.W.Hasluck)
1923. The Significance of Greek Personal
Names. FOLKLORE 34: 149-54.

This article describes the system for naming
children after living and dead relatives, and
the significance for the dead person's soul.
Based on study in Kastoria, an isolated region
in western Macedonia.

171 Hasluck, Margaret M. (Margaret M.Hardie)
1927. The Basil-Cake of the Greek New Year.
FOLKLORE 38: 143-177.

This study of the New Year basil cake,
examines its use in the New Year's
celebration: how it is cut and eaten, the
history of the cake and ceremony, and legends
associated with it. Comparisons with similar
food traditions in other countries are also
made.

172 Haxthausen, Werner von
1935. NEUGRIECHISCHE VOLKSLIEDER. Ed. Karl
Schulte Kemminghausen and Gustav Soyter.
Münster: Aschendorff. 195 pp.

Greek texts with German translations on
opposite pages of ninety-eight songs and
seventy-one distichs. The songs are mainly
from Northern Greece and the Ionian Islands
collected from Greeks in Europe in 1814 but
not published until 1935.

173 Hepding, Hugo

1923. Einige neugriechischen Schwänke.
LAOGRAPHIA 7: 304-314.

In 1913 and 1917 the author collected funny
stories from Greek military personnel
stationed in the Greek islands. This article
includes a brief commentary and notes on
origin of the stories in German and the text
of eleven short funny stories in Greek.
References are made to similar stories
published elsewhere in LAOGRAPHIA.

174 Herzfeld, Michael
1971. Cost and Culture: Observations on
Incised Cement Decorations in Crete. KRETIKA
CHRONIKA [Cretan Chronicles] 23: 189-198.

A study of the cement decorations in the
Cretan city of Rethymnon and a nearby
village. When asked by the author to explain
these designs some inhabitants gave elaborate
symbolic interpretations; others said there
was nothing symbolic about them. Illustrated
with photographs.

175 Herzfeld, Michael
1973. "The Siege of Rhodes" and the
Ethnography of Greek Oral Tradition. KRETIKA
CHRONIKA [Cretan Chronicles] 25: 413-440.

An examination of the text of one Cretan
folksong and its position within the wider
fields of literature and folk tradition of
Greece.

176 Herzfeld, Michael
1974. Cretan Distichs: "The Quartered Shield"
in a Cross-Cultural Perspective. SEMIOTICA 12:
203-218.

The purpose of this article is to test a model

of semantic taxonomy on the proverbial rhymed
distich in order to better understand the
ethnography of oral tradition. To effect the
test Herzfeld worked on a collection of 353
Cretan rhyming distichs, or mantinadhes, as
well as material he himself had collected.
The Greek and English texts of several
mantinadhes are included.

177 Herzfeld, Michael
    1977. Ritual and Textual Structures: The
    Advent of Spring in Rural Greece. In TEXT AND
    CONTEXT: THE SOCIAL ANTHROPOLOGY OF TRADITION,
    ed.Ravindra K. Jain. pp.29-50. A.S.A.Essays
    2. Philadelphia: Institute for the Study of
    Human Issues.

    This essay is based on the author's study of a
    spring ritual in two rural areas of Rhodes as
    well as data on similar rites in the northern
    mainland. The ritual mediates the symbolic
    and actual transition from winter to spring,
    and involves singing, carrying a ritual
    object, and going from house to house. The
    songs are called swallow songs or kheldonisma,
    and each village has its own song. A series
    of variant texts of kheldonisma are examined.
    This article shows the importance of studying
    folklore in its context.

178 Herzfeld, Michael
    1979. Exploring a Metaphor of Exposure.
    JOURNAL OF AMERICAN FOLKLORE 92: 285-301.

    Herzfeld states that metaphor is an
    encapsulation of paradox. In this article he
    examines a metaphor which connects male
    genitals with the Epitaphios, a very holy icon
    depicting Christ entombed. He contends that
    although sexual humor is not uncommon there is
    no place for sexuality in the national
    examination of folklore. Sexuality at the

local level is suppressed but exists. This article is based on fieldwork in a small island near Rhodes in 1974, specifically on the Good Friday celebration in which the icon is prominent, and on couplets called mantinadhes, in which this sexuality is evident.

179 Herzfeld, Michael
1980. Social Borderers: Themes of Conflict and Ambiguity in Greek Folk-Song. BYZANTINE AND MODERN GREEK STUDIES 6: 61-80.

This article examines four songs with similar themes--e.g., birth, mother, rapid growth, meeting/confrontation with father--to the Akritic songs. Songs are in Greek and English.

180 Herzfeld, Michael
1981. An Indigenous Theory of Meaning and its Elicitation in Performative Context. SEMIOTICA 34: 113-141.

Based on fieldwork in a village in Rhodes in 1973-74, this article examines mantinadhes, the Greek word for distichs. In analyzing mantinadhes, Herzfeld finds that their significance lies in context which can be verbal, circumstantial or social. Forty-four mantinadhes are studied, with text in both Greek and English. Detailed context for use as provided by informants is given.

181 Herzfeld, Michael
1981. Meaning and Morality: A Semantic Approach to Evil Eye Accusations in a Greek Village. AMERICAN ETHNOLOGIST 8: 560-574.

This article is based on the author's fieldwork in a Rhodian village in 1973-74 and

includes a review of the ethnographic
literature on the evil eye in Greece. Herzfeld
analyzes the behavior of those accused of
giving the evil eye as well as that of their
accusers, and finds a system dealing with
insiders and outsiders. Boundary
transgression is tied up in the conceptual
system of evil eye belief. Case studies of
four people who are outsiders and believed by
villagers to be people who might cast the evil
eye illustrate that evil eye belief is more
complex and far reaching than it seems.

182 Herzfeld, Michael
    1981. Performative Categories and Symbols of
    Passage in Rural Greece. JOURNAL OF AMERICAN
    FOLKLORE 94: 44-57.

    In examining the surprising similarities in
    texts of wedding songs and moirologhia
    (mourning songs), the author finds the
    similarities to be logical when death and
    marriage are seen as rites of passage. This
    article stresses the importance of studying
    songs in their context and labels the attempts
    of earlier folklorists to classify songs as
    too simplistic. The text of many songs
    recorded by the author in 1972 are included.

183 Herzfeld, Michael
    1982. OURS ONCE MORE: FOLKLORE, IDEOLOGY AND
    THE MAKING OF GREECE. Austin: University of
    Texas. 197 pp.

    This book examines the development of folklore
    study in Greece and its relationship to the
    Greek nation as it emerged from centuries of
    Ottoman domination, in the nineteenth century,
    to the destruction of Smyrna and collapse of
    the Megali Idhea. Much of Greek folklore
    scholarship was expended on looking backwards
    and proving that the inhabitants of the modern

nation were descendants of ancient Greece. Folktales, songs, art, and ritual were all examined as survivals from antiquity to prove to non-believers and foreign interests that the modern Greeks were not Slavs but the rightful heirs to the entire Greek-speaking world, the dream of the Megali Idhea. The work and political significance of specific folklorists, in particular Nikolaos Politis, is dicussed is detail. Two useful appendices are included: 1) Politis' Folklore Taxonomy, which classifies the areas appropriate for folklore research, according to the founder of Greek folklore study, and 2) Basic Chronolgy, which shows parallel chronologies of Greek political history, folklore stories and European and related studies.

184 Herzfeld, Michael
1983. Semantic Slippage and Moral Fall: The Rhetoric of Chastity in Rural Greek Society. JOURNAL OF MODERN GREEK STUDIES 1: 161-172.

Based on Herzfeld's 1974 fieldwork, this article examines the complaint that Greek village women are not as chaste as they were in earlier times and its relationship to the claim that the exotika (supernatural creatures) no longer exist because no one believes in them. He points out the importance of context, in this case, cultural context, in understanding these statements as symbolic rather than real.

185 Hionis, Peri
1977. Greek Folk Tales. NEW JERSEY FOLKLORE 1(2): 8-11.

Three folktales collected by the author. Includes names of informants and description of informants' emotional involvement with the stories.

186 Hoeg, Carsten
   1925-26. LES SARAKATSANS: UNE TRIBE NOMADE
   GRECQUE. Paris: Champion. 2 vols. 312 pp.,
   212 pp.

   This thesis is based on two months in 1922
   that the author spent with the Sarakatsans, a
   nomadic tribe of northern Greece, and a
   follow-up visit in 1924. Volume one is a
   linguistic study of the tribe's dialect and
   includes photographs, a description of the
   people, and some discussion of material
   culture, customs and folklore. The second
   volume includes texts of eighteen tales and
   sixty songs in modern Greek with French
   summaries.

187 Hoerburger, Felix
   1966. Beobachtungen Volkstanz in
   Nordgriechenland. ZEITSCHRIFT FUR VOLKSKUNDE
   62: 43-66.

   Observations of folkdance in Northern Greece,
   this article looks at the variety of dances,
   including those of Anatolia, round dances, the
   place of dance in the Anastenaria, and dance
   music. There is a lengthy section on rebetiko
   dances. Method of documentation of dance and
   its problems are discussed.

188 Hoerburger, Felix
   1967. Oriental Elements in the Folk Dance and
   Folk Dance Music of Greek Macedonia. JOURNAL
   OF THE INTERNATIONAL FOLK MUSIC COUNCIL 19:
   71-75.

   This article examines mainly Turkish names,
   origins, and instruments of folkdance music,
   e.g., rebetiko, dances of Greek refugees of
   Asia Minor, and the dances of the Anastenaria.

Some dances are described.

189 Holden, Ricky and Mary Vouras
    1965. GREEK FOLK DANCES. Newark, NJ: Folkraft,
    1965. 128 pp.

    This book gives instructions, music and
    background notes for eighty-six Greek
    folkdances. A brief introduction includes
    choreography, count, instruments, rhythms, and
    geographical origin. A bibliography on Greek
    folkdance is included.

190 Holst, Gail
    1977. ROAD TO REMBETIKA: MUSIC FROM A GREEK
    SUB-CULTURE; SONGS OF LOVE, SORROW AND
    HASHISH. 2nd ed. Athens: Anglo-Hellenic Publ.
    176 pp.

    This book is the author's late-1960s search
    for rebetiko and rebetes. The history of the
    rebetiko revival is examined as well as the
    performers, instruments, dance and verse
    styles. A comparison to American urban blues
    is made and the historical and sociological
    forces that shaped rebetiko are discussed.
    The lyrics of eighty-three selected songs in
    Greek and English translation are given, with
    type of dance, composer when known, and date.
    A bibliography, a discography, and indexes by
    first line, title, and subject are also
    included.

191 Holton, D.W.
    1975. "The Leprous Queen"--A Ballad from
    Lesbos. BYZANTINE AND MODERN GREEK STUDIES 1:
    97-109.

    This article studies the history of a song
    collected in Lesbos in the late 1950's. The
    text of the ballad and part of the score are

included.

192 Horalek, Karel
1965 Le specimen folklorique du roman byzantin
"Kallimachos et Chrysorrhoe." LAOGRAPHIA 22:
174-178.

This article examines the Byzantine poem,
"Kallimachos and Chrysorrhoe," for folkloric
content and compares it to modern folktales.

193 Imellos, Stephen D.
1980. Das Lied vom Schwimmer unde seine
Herkunft. BALKAN STUDIES 21: 217-231.

This article studies the "Song of the
Swimmer," a folksong found in northern Greece.
Texts of variants in Greek are included.

194 Ioannides, Costas D.
1968. A Short Collection of Cyprus Folksongs.
KYPRIAKAI SPOUDAI [Cypriot Studies] 32:
265-300.

Examples of songs in sixteen subject
categories from tape-recordings in the
archives of the Cyprus Research Center. The
lyrics are given in Greek with English
summaries.

195 Ioannides, Costas D.
1973. Singing Games. KYPRIAKAI SPOUDAI
[Cypriot Studies] 37: 30-60.

Gives texts of seventeen singing games played
by children (mainly girls) and religious
singing games performed by adults. Musical
scores, lyrics and translation of lyrics are
given for each song as well as context.

196 Ioannidou-Barbarigou, M.
1965. Classification des legendes populaires
grecques. LAOGRAPHIA 22: 179-184.

This paper describes a system used in Greece
for classifying legends which was first
developed by Nikolaos Politis, then refined by
Stilpon Kyriakides and other folklorists.

197 Jaffe, Grace M.
1957. Folkways and Mores in a Greek-American
Community. TRANSACTIONS OF THE ILLINOIS STATE
ACADEMY OF SCIENCE 45: 148-54.

A slightly condescending article by a
sociologist who focuses on the experiences of
two recent immigrants to the United States.

198 Jeannaraki, Anton
1967. ASMATA KRETIKA META DISTICHON KAI
PAROIMION [Kretan Songs with Couplets and
Proverbs]. Wiesbaden: Sandig. 386 pp.
(Original: Kretas Volkslieder nebst Distichen
und Sprichwörten. Leipzig: Brockhaus, 1876.)

One of the first publications of Greek
folksongs, this book includes 317 songs, 258
mantinadhes or couplets, and 201 proverbs.
Also included is a Greek-German glossary.

199 Johnstone, Pauline
1961. GREEK ISLAND EMBROIDERY. London:
Tiranti. 58 pp.

This book is an illustrated guide to
embroidery from the Greek islands.

200 Jones, Louis C.
1951. The Evil-Eye among European-Americans.

WESTERN FOLKLORE 10: 11-25.

This article is based on material collected by
the author's folklore students at the New York
State College for Teachers between 1940-1946.
Beliefs about the evil eye among many European
groups, including Greek-Americans, are
discussed.

201 Kakouri, Katerina I.
1956. "Droměna" Champětres. Le "Leidinos." Une
représentation Dramatique de Magie Populaire
en Grèce. L'HELLENISME CONTEMPORAIN, ser.2,
annee 10: 188-212.

The Leidinos is a rural ritual ceremony, or
dromenon, celebrated on September 14, on the
island of Aegina. The author visited many
villages in Aegina to observe the ceremony and
collect data on it. Each village has its own
version but it is now mainly acted out by
children who dress, transport, and tear the
effigy of a dead youth. The legends of
Leidinos, customs and food associated with it,
and songs sung are included in a detailed
description of the ceremony. The author
believes it descended from pre-Christian
beliefs, possibly an Adonis cult. Conflict
between official religion and this kind of
practice caused many customs associated with
it to be lost.

202 Kakouri, Katerina I.
1965. DEATH AND RESURRECTION; CONCERNING
DRAMATIZED CEREMONIES OF THE GREEK POPULAR
WORSHIP. Translated by W.D.Cousin. Athens:
G.C.Elefteroudakis. 46 pp.

Dromena are sacred, dramatized ceremonies of
worship. This book describes in detail four
dromena of death and destruction from the
Zagori region in Epirus: 1) the Passion of

Saint Christos, 2) Lazarica--the raising of
Lazarus, 3) the Dead Man in the Pit, and 4)
the Zapheires. These dromena involve either an
effigy or a man imitating a dead body who are
raised from the dead. Mainly based on
published research, this work is illustrated
with photographs and drawings.

203 Kakouri, Katerina I.
    1965. DIONYSIAKA: ASPECTS OF POPULAR THRACIAN
    RELIGION OF TODAY. Translated by Helen
    Coloclides. Athens: G.C.Eleftheroudakis. 174
    pp. (Original: Dionysiaka, Athens, 1963.)

    This book is based on the author's research
    and observations begun in 1951 till the time
    of publication, as well as on unpublished
    material from the Athens Folklore Archives,
    and is an abridged version of her dissertation
    which was published in Greek. Kakouri had the
    book translated to make more widely known two
    related Thracian religious customs believed to
    be descended from the ancient Dionysian cult:
    1) the rites of the Anastenaria and 2) the
    dance/drama of the Kalogheros. The first part
    describes the practices surrounding these
    customs in detail, and includes the author's
    own eye-witness account of the Anastenaria.
    The second is the author's commentary on the
    two rituals, including discussion of their
    relationship, analysis of each, and evolution
    from Greek Dionysian worship. Illustrated
    with many drawings and photographs.

204 Kakrides, Johannes Theoph.
    1967. DIE ALTEN HELLENEN IM NEUGRIECHISCHEN
    VOLKSGLAUBEN. Munich: Heimeran. 88 pp.

    This three-part book deals with classical
    myths and historical tales that survived to
    the present in oral tradition. Kakrides
    examines why certain survivals persist and how

they are changed to fit the folk imagination.

205 Kaloyanides, Michael G.
    1977. New York and Bouzoukia: The Rise of
    Greek-American Music. ESSAYS IN ARTS AND
    SCIENCES 6: 95-103.

    This article discusses changes in Greek music
    as its identity moves from a regional base to
    a national one. Greek and Greek-American
    music are briefly compared.

206 Kavvadias, Georigos B.
    1965. PASTEURS-NOMADES MEDITERRANEENS: LES
    SARACATSANS DE GRECE. Paris: Gauthier-Villars.
    444 pp.

    An ethnography of the Sarakatsans, a tribe of
    northern Greece, including data on religious
    and magic beliefs and customs. Illustrated
    with many photographs.

207 Kenna, Margaret E.
    1976. Houses, Fields and Graves: Property and
    Ritual Obligation on a Greek Island. ETHNOLOGY
    15: 21-34.

    This mainly ethnographic study, based on 16
    months on a Cycladic island in 1966-67, has a
    section on the fate of the soul. Included are
    phrases uttered about the dead, description of
    memorial services, and discussion of food made
    for the memorial and exhumation services. The
    author finds a connection between property and
    obligation to the souls of the property
    owners.

208 Kenna, Margaret E.
    1977. Greek Urban Migrants and the Rural
    Patron Saint. ETHNIC STUDIES 1: 14-23.

This article, based on 1966-67 fieldwork with
400 inhabitants of a fictitious island, Nisos,
and 1973 fieldwork among Nisiot migrants to
Athens, studies the cult of a local saint.
The author finds that the cult of Panayia
Kalamiotissa, especially prayers and vows,
helps to unite migrants.

209 Kiriazis, James W.
1971. Folklore and Cultural Character.
BULLETIN OF THE PENNSYLVANIA STATE MODERN
LANGUAGE ASSOCIATION 49(no.1-2): 8-16.

.Discusses use of folklore, especially
folktales, in childrearing practices of four
cultures--Polish, Zuni, Chinese and Rhodian
Greek--for developing personality and cultural
character.

210 Kosmetatou, Helene
1976. THE HISTORY OF RURAL AND URBAN COSTUME
IN CEPHALONIA. Argostoli, Cephalonia:
Corgialenios Museum. 83 pp.

This museum publication traces the development
of Kephalonian costume from 1500 onward.
Kephalonia was occupied by the Venetians,
French, and British, and many elements of
European clothes were adapted to suit the
island's way of life. Illustrated with
photographs of the Museum's extensive costume
and photograph collection. Includes draft
patterns of actual costumes.

211 Koster, Joan Bouza
1976. From Spindle to Loom: Weaving in the
Southern Argolid. EXPEDITION 19(1): 29-39.

Description of weaving and the different
techniques of spindle design. The author

interviewed women about weaving and found that
loom weaving is dying out, and most girls find
the spindle and distaff old-fashioned.
Included are photographs of shearing,
spinning, washing wool, and weaving.

212 Koumoulides, John T.A.
1973. SUMMER IN A GREEK VILLAGE: STUDENT
ESSAYS ABOUT LIFE AND CUSTOMS IN A GREEK
VILLAGE. Muncie, Indiana: Ball State
University Press. 68 pp.

These essays by American and British
university students are based on their 1972
stay in a village in Thessaly. The purpose of
the visit was to learn about Greek village
community life. Customs, church services, and
festivals are described. Photographs
illustrate the essays.

213 Koussiadis, Giorgios A.
1952. Les danses populaires grecque.
L'HELLENISME CONTEMPORAIN, ser.2, année 6:
526-532.

In showing the evolution of Greek dance from
antiquity to modern folk dances, dances from
various parts of Greece are described and
compared. Positions and steps are outlined
and dances are categorized.

214 Kyriakides, Stilpon P.
1920. E GUNAIKES EIS TEN LAOGRAPHIAN. E LAIKE
POIETRIA--E PARAMYTHOU--E MAGISSA [Women in
Folklore. The Folk Poet--The Storyteller--The
Witch.]. Athens: Sidera. 152 pp.

This book is actually four conference papers
studying the role of women in Greek folklore
as seen in songs, tales, and magic.

215 Kyriakides, Stilpon P.
1922. ELLENIKE LAOGRAPHIA, MNEMEIA TOU LOGOU
[Greek Folklore, Monuments of Folk
Literature]. Demosievmata Laographikou
Archeiou, 3. Athens: Sakellariou. 446 pp.

The purpose of this work is to provide a
general idea of Greek folklore research,
including its themes, collections, and
systematic character. Kyriakides surveys the
entire area of Greek folkloristics. Each
chapter is devoted to a particular aspect of
study with an introductory discussion on how
it should be approached.

216 Kyriakides, Stilpon P.
1923. N.G.Politis. LAOGRAPHIA 7: ix-li.

This obituary of the father of Greek folklore
describes Politis and his role in folklore
studies. It includes a bibliography of all of
Politis' works.

217 Kyriakides, Stilpon P.
1931. Le folklore en Grèce de 1919 à 1930.
BYZANTION 7: 737-770.

For 1919-1930, this chronology briefly
summarizes folklore activity in Greece, e.g.,
journals, societies, etc., then lists
publications with brief descriptions of
periodical articles and books.

218 Kyriakides, Stilpon P.
1931. Gli Studi Folkloristici. LARES 2(2):
11-13.

This article briefly outlines the events which
made folklore a science in Greece. Before
folklore became an established and officially

recognized field of academic pursuit, with
university courses and scholarly socieities,
work was being done with Greek folkloric
materials by scholars whose interests were
primarily philological, archaeological or
patriotic. Kyriakides traces these endeavors
and notes initial publications and the
scholars (many of whom were foreign) involved.

219 Kyriakides, Stilpon P.
    1938-48. Ti einai Laographia, kai eis ti
    Dunati na Ophelese e Spoude tes [What is
    Folklore and What ends can the Study of it
    Serve?]. LAOGRAPHIA 12: 130-157.

    In this important article Kyriakides surveys
    folklore studies in other countries as well as
    Greece. He emphasizes the importance of
    recognizing that folklore is always changing.

220 Kyriakides, Stilpon P.
    1968. TWO STUDIES OF MODERN GREEK FOLKLORE.
    Hetaireia Makedonikon Spoudon.Hidryma Meleton
    Chersonesou tou Haimou, 97. Thessaloniki:
    Institute for Balkan Studies. 132 pp.

    "Modern Greek Folklore: Folk Poetry, Folk
    Religion, and Folk Art, with References to
    German Folklore (With Illustrations)," is the
    text of a lecture delivered in 1936
    ["Neugriechische Volkskunde. Volksdichtung,
    Volksglaube..." Thessalonike]. This student of
    Politis, the father of modern Greek folklore,
    discusses some examples of Greek folk poetry,
    religion and art with comparisons to German
    eqivalents.
    "The Language and Folk Culture of Modern
    Greece," was originally written in 1943
    [Glossa kai Laikos Politismos ton Neoteron
    Ellenikon. Athens. 1946.] in reaction to Nazi
    insinuations that modern Greeks were merely
    descendants of barbaric Slavic tribes. The
    author examines folk language, general folk

culture, material culture, folk beliefs and folk poetry, and stresses their evolution from classical and Byzantine Greece. In both essays he points out the lack of studies in such important areas as folk art, folk architecture and clothing, but emphasizes the overall continuity from the past to the present.

221 Kyriakidou-Nestoros, Alke
1963. Folk Art in Greek Macedonia. BALKAN STUDIES 4(1-2): 15-36.

This article documents folk art in Macedonia from the 19th century to the present, briefly describing all crafts. The development and establishment of the Folklore Museum of· Northern Greece and the Folklore Museum of the University of Thessaloniki are traced by the author, a folklorist at the University of Thessaloniki.

222 Kyriakidou-Nestoros, Alke
1964. The IV International Congress for Folk Narrative Research. BALKAN STUDIES 5: 323-327.

The author summarizes the proceedings of this congress (Athens, September 1-6, 1964) which compared ancient Greek tradition with modern Greek folklore.

223 Kyriakidou-Nestoros, Alke
1972. The Study of Folklore in Greece: Laographia in its Contemporary Perspective. EAST EUROPEAN QUARTERLY 5: 487-504.

A discussion of the changing notion of folklore and the folk which defines folklore as the study of traditional culture. The author finds that a problem with Greek folklore study has been the emphasis on proving that modern Greek custom, ritual, belief, etc., have their roots in classical antiquity.

224 Kyriakidou-Nestoros, Alke
1975. LAOGRAPHIKA MELETEMATA [Folkloric Studies]. Athens: Ekdoseis Olkos. 269 pp.

This book reprints various articles and reviews by Alke Kyriakidou-Nestoros, a folklorist at the University of Thessaloniki. The articles are on three topics: 1) use of space in traditional culture, 2) folklore theories, including the study of folklore in Greece, and 3) specific subjects of folklore study.

225 Kyriakidou-Nestoros, Alke
1978. E THEORIA TES ELLENIKES LAOGRAPHIAS, KRITIKE ANALYSE [The Theory of Greek Folklore, Critical Analysis]. Athens: Hetairea Spoudon Neoellenikou Politismou kai Genikes Paideias. 233 pp.

This study on Greek folklore theory, by an important contemporary Greek folklorist, divides its topic into two sections: Part 1 deals with the romantic interpretation of nation and folklore, as well as the scientific phase of Greek folklore. Part 2 covers folkloric method including folklore and archaeology, Politis and the comparative method, Kyriakides and the historical method, and the relationship between the people and folklore.

226 Kyriakidou-Nestoros, Maria-Alke
1982. Oral History and Folklore. In NEW TRENDS IN MODERN GREEK HISTORIOGRAPHY, ed.A.Lily Macrakis and P.Nikiforos Diamandouros. pp.1-5. Hanover, NH: Modern Greek Studies

Association in cooperation with Anatolia College.

This paper, which was presented at a history symposium, describes the themes covered in Kyriakidou-Nestoros' University of Thessaloniki seminar on oral history and folklore. She states that oral history belongs to history and folklore, and that the relationship between the two disciplines is important.

227 Lake, H.Coote
    1931. Mummers' Plays and the Sacer Ludus.
    FOLKLORE 42: 141-149.

    This article focuses on English mummers plays and compares them to Thracian plays as described by Dawkins in 1906 (JOURNAL OF HELLENIC STUDIES 26: 191-206). Described and examined are the six sequences of events: contest, death, speech, lamentation, recognition and resurrection.

228 Lampsidis, Od.
    1965. Contribution à l'étude des contes populaires des Grecs du Ponte-Euxin (Asie Mineure). LAOGRAPHIA 22: 213-216.

    This paper briefly describes religous elements in stories from Pontus, mainly based on work done by the Commission for Pontic Studies, founded in 1927.

229 Lang, Andrew
    1900. Medical Superstition in Cyprus. FOLKLORE 11: 120-125.

    An account of an 1899 court case in Larnaca, Cyprus, which shows active belief in the curative powers of a snake's horn.

230 Lawson, John Cuthbert
    1899-1900. A Beast-Dance in Skyros. ANNUAL OF
    THE BRITISH SCHOOL OF ATHENS 6: 125-127.

    This article is a brief description of the
    pre-Lenten festival which incluldes the
    Kalogheri: shepherds who dress in goat hides
    and bells and perform an ancient dance.

231 Lawson, John Cuthbert
    1964. MODERN GREEK FOLKLORE AND ANCIENT GREEK
    RELIGION. Hyde Park, NY: University Books. 620
    pp. (Original: Cambridge University Press,
    1910.)

    The purpose of this work was to prove that
    customs and beliefs survived from ancient
    Greece to modern times. Lawson did his
    research in 1898-1900, not by means of formal
    interview techniques but simply by talking
    with Greek villagers. In examining modern
    folklore Lawson saw continuity from pagan
    tradition on to the present. Chapters are
    devoted to pagan deities, e.g., Charon, Pan,
    the Nymphs; soul and body, e.g., vampires,
    revenants, superstitions; and cremation,
    dissolution, and gods and men. He compares
    literature and folksong, art and folk art,
    ancient and modern customs. His discovery of
    similarities between modern and ancient
    religious practices was revolutionary at the
    time of publication.

232 Lee, Dorothy Demetracopoulou
    1936. Folklore of the Greeks in America.
    FOLKLORE 47: 294-310.

    In 1934-35 the author collected folktales and
    beliefs about the supernatural from immigrants
    from Pontus, Lesbos and Arcadia who settled in

Massachusetts. She found that the women, whom
she called the guardians of tradition, were
eager to talk to her but the men were not
willing initially. Since life is so different
in America folktales are destined to die.

233 Lee, Dorothy D.
1942. Greek Accounts of the Vrykolakas.
JOURNAL OF AMERICAN FOLKLORE 55: 126-132.

The author collected stories about the
non-human vampire-like Vrykolakas from Greek
immigrants in Massachusetts. The informants
did not distinguish these accounts as fact or
fiction.

234 Lee, Dorothy D.
1946. Greek Tales of Nastradi Hodjas. FOLKLORE
57: 188-197.

Twenty-nine stories from Constantinople, west
Asia Minor, and Pontus collected from Turkish
Greeks in the Boston area in 1934 and 1937.
The Hodjas was a poor Turkish priest-teacher
who both played tricks and was the butt of
jokes.

235 Lee, Dorothy D.
1947. Greek Tales of Priests and Priestwife.
JOURNAL OF AMERICAN FOLKLORE 60: 163-167.

These nine tales collected in the Boston area
in 1934 and 1937 show the ambivalence Greeks
feel toward priests who are figures of both
respect and ridicule.

236 Lee, Dorothy D.
1951 Greek Personal Accounts of the
Supernatural. JOURNAL OF AMERICAN FOLKLORE 64:
307-312.

Accounts of various supernatural creatures
including the Dracos, Baboulas, Spanoi, and
Vaskania, told to the author by seven Greeks
from Lesbos or Arcadia. The informants
displayed varying degrees of belief in the
tales.

237 Lee, Dorothy D.
1951. Three Romances from Pontus. FOLKLORE 62:
388-397, 449-453.

These three tales, which are the type that
were told by wandering minstrels in coffee
houses in Pontus, were told to the author by
an immigrant from Pontus.

238 Lee, Dorothy
1953. Greece. In CULTURAL PATTERNS AND
TECHNICAL CHANGE, ed.Margaret Mead.
pp.77-114. Paris: UNESCO.

This survey of Greek culture is based on
interviews and correspondence during 1950-51,
as well as examinations of child care manuals
and collections of folksongs. Upon
examination of attitudes toward work, time,
self and responsibility and the state of
nutrition, health care, child care and
religion, the author predicts problems with
social change.

239 Legrand, Emile
1874. RECUEIL DE CHANSONS POPULAIRES GRECS.
Paris: Maisonneuve. 376 pp.

This book is a collection of five songs and
100 distichs in Greek and French by one of the
first Frenchmen to study modern Greek language
and folklore.

240 Legrand, Emile
    1881. RECUEIL DE CONTES POPULAIRES GRECS.
    Paris: Leroux. 144 pp.

    This book includes thirty Greek folktales
    translated into French.

241 Litsas, F.K.
    1976. Rousalia: The Ritual Worship of the
    Dead. In THE REALM OF THE EXTRA-HUMAN: AGENTS
    AND AUDIENCES, ed.Agehananda Bharati.
    pp.447-465. The Hague: Mouton.

    The author states that the Rousalia rituals
    are the most representative and widely
    practiced celebrations for honoring the dead
    in Greece today. The souls of Sinners in Hell
    are allowed to come to earth for fifty days,
    from Easter to Pentecost, and Rousalia is the
    last day of the fifty. This article, which is
    based on research in the southwestern
    Pelopennesus and western Macedonia, examines
    the various rituals surrounding Rousalia Day
    which include special foods, exhumation of
    remains with predictions based on the
    condition of the bones, and performance of
    elegies. This study shows both survivals from
    antiquity and current attitudes toward death.

242 Lord, Albert B.
    1976. The Heroic Tradition of Greek Epic and
    Ballad: Continuity and Change. In HELLENISM
    AND THE FIRST GREEK WAR OF LIBERATION
    (1821-1830): CONTINUITY AND CHANGE, ed.
    Nikiforos P.Diamandouros et al. pp.79-94.
    Thessaloniki: Institute for Balkan Studies.

    This well-known scholar of oral tradition
    studies some songs from the Notopoulos
    collection of tapes and manuscripts of modern
    Greek music and song at Harvard in order to

identify elements of narrative song that have
lasted from antiquity to modern times. He
discusses a song from the Akritic cycle, a
Cretan historical song, and a klephtic song,
and concludes that songs change as a result of
religious, social, political and linguistic
changes.

243 Loukatos, D.S.
1951. RELIGION POPULAIRE A CEPHALONIE.
Collection de l'Institut Français d'Athènes,
no.45. Athens: Institut Français d'Athènes.
221 pp.

This study is actually a religious testimonial
to the Ionian island of Kephalonia based on
the author's childhood memories. Histories of
individual churches and clergy, festivals of
patron saints, religious curiosities are
described in detail. A detailed map of the
island is included as well as 28
illustrations.

244 Loukatos, D.S.
1951. La traditions populaires et l'unité du
caractere Grec. L'HELLENISME CONTEMPORAIN,
ser.2, année 5: 51-58.

This article outlines the history of the study
of folklore in Greece, names important
scholars in folklore and related areas, and
describes the folklore archives at the Academy
of Athens. Loukatos sees popular tradition as
intact and continuing.

245 Loukatos, Demetrios
1952. Curiosities cultuelles à Cephalonie.
L'HELLENISME CONTEMPORAIN, ser.2, année 6:
57-64.

This article provides descriptive accounts of

two local religious festivals from villages in
Cephalonia: August 14, festival of serpents,
and August 16, procession of St. Gerasime.

246 Loukatos, Demetrios
1956-57. Ellenika Ethnographika Antikeimena
sto Musee de l'Hommo tou Parisou [Hellenic
Ethnographic Artifacts in the Musée de l'Homme
in Paris]. In MELANGES OFFERTS A OCTAVE ET
MELPO MERLIER A L'OCCASION DU 25E ANNIVERSAIRE
DE LEUR ARRIVEE EN GRECE, vol.2. pp.27-42.
Athens: L'Institut Français d'Athènes.

This article describes the collection of Greek
folk art, jewelry and costume in the Musée de
l'Homme, in Paris. The artifacts are described
with a history about their purpose in being at
the museum. Illustrated with photographs.

247 Loukatos, Demetrios
1957. NEOELLENIKA LAOGRAPHIKA Keimena [Modern
Greek Folklore Texts]. Athens: Zacharopoulou.
331 pp.

This collection includes 252 Greek folktales
with Aarne-Thompson tale types given.

248 Loukatos, Demetrios
1965. L'emploi du proverbe aux differents
ages. PROVERBIUM 2: 17-26.

In studying proverb use by different age
groups, the author found that older people use
them the most. This article includes more
than fifty Greek proverbs in French.

249 Loukatos, Demetrios
1965. Le Proverbe dans le Conte. LAOGRAPHIA
22: 229-233.

This paper finds the use of proverbs in Greek
folk narratives dependent on five factors: 1)
region, 2) storyteller, 3) nature of the tale,
4) time, and 5) the investigation about the
proverb.

250 Loukatos, Demetrios
1967. Wellerismes latents. PROVERBIUM 9:
193-196.

In this article modern Greek Wellerisms are
divided into three categories to illustrate
how latent Wellerisms are a specific
sub-category. Includes text of thirty-two
Wellerisms.

251 Loukatos, Demetrios
1971. Proverbes grecs (neohelléniques) en
langues etrangères (Choix de bibliographie
depuis 1800). PROVERBIUM 16: 588-589.

A bibliography of English, German, and French
books on modern Greek proverbs.

252 Loukatos, Demetrios
1972. Etat actuel des études folkloriques en
Grèce. ACTES DU IIE CONGRES INTERNATIONAL DES
ETUDES DU SUD-EST EUROPEEN, ATHENES, 7-13 MAI,
1970. A: 551-582.

A study of the history and current state of
Greek folklore studies by a pre-eminent Greek
folklorist, this article first examines the
history of Greek folklore in five periods.
The second section covers the development of
folklore societies, periodicals, archives,
research centers, academic instruction,
museums, and other organizations. The third
part discusses sources and subjects of
folklore research in Greece, methods and
instruments, and the relationship of folklore

to other disciplines. The final section is a
desiderata list. Since much of Greek folklore
scholarship has been carried out for a
national purpose, Loukatos would like to see
more independent research. Also shows more
concern for preservation of survivals than
current folk behavior, in particular, effects
of tourism on "true" folklore,

253 Loukatos, Demetrios
1976. Personification of Capes and Rocks in
the Hellenic Seas. In THE REALM OF THE
EXTRA-HUMAN: AGENTS AND AUDIENCES,
ed.Agehananda Bharati. pp.467-474. The Hague:
Mouton.

A collection of Greek maritime folklore. The
author believes that personification imposed
on inanimate objects is based on man's need
for a milieu of human-like beings. Legends
usually accompany such names. Types of names
that refer to parts of the human body,
animals, etc., are listed for 1) capes and
promontories, and 2) rocks and islets. This
use of toponymies is dying out.

254 Loukatos, Demetrios
1978. EISAGOGE STIN ELLENIKE LAOGRAPHIA
[Introduction to Greek Folklore]. Athens:
Morphotiko Idrima Ellenikes Trapezis. 351 pp.

This book traces the history of Greek folklore
and the major areas of folklore research in
Greece: philological and customs, including
social traditions, rites of passage, physical
and metaphysical states, and popular worship.
There are bibliographies, of research
publications mainly in Greek, at the end of
each section.

255 Loukatos, Demetrios

1978. Tourist Archeofolklore in Greece. In
FOLKLORE IN THE MODERN WORLD, ed.Richard
M.Dorson. pp.175-182. The Hague: Mouton.

Loukatos examines the evolution of the popular
movement which developed an awareness of
Greekness. This lead to archaeologically-
inspired crafts or "archaeofolklore" which he
sees as a segment of urban folklore. This
borrowing from the past stimulates tourism
which encourages production of such articles.

256 Loukatos, Demetrios
1981. Narrateurs d'Equippage sur les Bateaux
Helleniques. FABULA 22: 90-95.

In discussing the storytelling behavior of
Greek sailors, Loukatos describes a time that
he says no longer exists. Before the advent
of radio and television, and before officers
and sailors were separated by rank, sea-faring
men told stories. The manners and gestures of
the storyteller, use of repetition and kinds
of tales preferred are discussed. Stories
told are becoming more international as
sailors in oil liners trade stories.

257 Loukopoulos, D. and D.Petropoulos
1949. E LAIKE LATREIA TON PHARASON. THE
POPULAR RELIGION OF FARASSA. Collection de
l'Institut Français d'Athènes, no.34. Athens:
L'Institut Français d'Athènes. 163 pp.

The Greek population of the Cappadocian town
of Farassa was the focus of numerous studies
of the Institut Francais because of its
geographical isolation. In this book, which
is written in Greek, some traditions and
religious beliefs are traced to antiquity.
The first section describes religious customs
and beliefs, churches, icons, healing, etc.
Part 2 summarizes winter and spring folk

customs.

258 Loukopoulos, D. and D.S.Loukatos
1951. PAROIMIES TON PHARASON. PROVERBS OF
FARASSA. Collection de l'Institut Français
d'Athènes, no.21. Athens: L' Institut
Français d'Athènes. 220 pp.

This book, written in Greek, contains 900
proverbs in original dialect with modern Greek
translation and notes. 662 were collected by
Loukopoulos before he died in 1943. The
remainder were contributed by Demetrios
Loukatos and Richard Dawkins. The proverbs are
arranged by subject or keyword, with name,
age, occupation, and residence of informant.
Glossary and bibliography are included.

259 Lüdeke, Hedwig
1949. Griechische Volksdichtung. ARCHIV FUR
LITERATUR UND VOLKSDICHTUNG 1: 196-250.

This important article is a thorough
examination of the history and state of Greek
folk poetry. It includes the text in German
of more than forty folksongs and distichs.
Some are from printed sources but most were
collected by the author. Name, age and
location of informant are provided.

260 Lykiardopoulos, Amica
1981. The Evil Eye: Towards an Exhaustive
Study. FOLKLORE 92: 221-230.

This comparative survey of the evil eye
includes many references to Greek culture. It
covers casting the evil eye, protection
against it, and detecting and curing its
effects.

261 MacCallum, Frank Lyman
1927. The Great Blessing. ASIA 27: 583-585.

A description of the blessing of the waters on
Epiphany morning in Constantinople.

262 MacDougall, Allan Ross
1942. AND THE GREEKS, A BOOK OF HELLENIC
RECIPES AND CULINARY LORE. New York: Near East
Foundation. 109 pp.

A book of recipes gathered in America and in
Greece, this work includes ethnographic and
historical data on food preparation and
cooking as well as commentary on Greek
foodways taken from travel accounts from the
16th century to the present.

263 MacMillan, Susan L.
1974. GREEK ISLAND EMBROIDERIES. Boston:
Museum of Fine Arts. 63 pp.

A catalog of the Museum of Fine Arts'
extensive collection of embroideries from
Greek islands, illustrated with color and
black and white photographs. Includes
discussion on the use of embroidery and the
history of regional activity.

264 Makres, Manoles
1983. DODEKANESIAKA DEMOTIKA TRAGOUDIA:
ANTHOLOGIA [Dodecanesian Popular Songs: An
Anthology]. Rhodos: Prisma. 351 pp.

This collection contains the text of 230 songs
of the Dodecanese islands, both from published
sources and collected by the author.
Arrangement is by type of song which includes
Akritic, narrative, historical, love, wedding,
lullabies, moirologhia, satirical, work, and

mantinadhes. The introduction lists published collections of folksongs of the Dodecanese by island with a brief history of folksong collecting in each island. For some songs references are given to parallels found in other islands. A glossary and a bibliography are included.

265 Mandel, Ruth
1983. Sacrifice at the Bridge of Arta: Sex Roles and the Manipulation of Power. JOURNAL OF MODERN GREEK STUDIES 1: 173-183.

Using symbolic and structural analysis, Mandel discusses female liminality and woman-as-sacrifical-victim, and shows that the famous ballad, "The Bridge of Arta," reflects the rural Greek attitudes toward woman as expendable, as well as showing her to be the necessary bridge between families and between the dead and the living.

266 Marangoni, Mario
1960. Alcune Tradizioni Popolari Vigenti nella Grecia del XXe Secolo. SOCIOLOGIA RELIGIOSA 5-6: 65-75.

This article discusses some folk traditions related to the life cycle or religious holidays and medical practices as seen in modern Greece in the 1950s. Occasionally ancient or other traditions are related.

267 Marinatos, Sp.
1965. On the Track of Folklore Elements in Bronze Age Art and Literature. LAOGRAPHIA 22: 262-273.

Although this article mainly examines folklore motifs in art and literature of the Bronze Age, there is some discussion of survivals of these folk themes into modern times.

268 Marinatos, Spyridon
1967. KLEIDUNG, HAAR-UND BARTTRACHT.
ARHAEOLOGIA HOMERICA: DIE DENKMALER UND DAS
FRUH GRIECHISCHE EPOS, Bd.I, Kap.A/B.
Göttingen: Vandenhoeck und Ruprecht. 113 pp.

The first part of an encylopedia on Homer as
seen in archaeology. Clothing, hair and beard
dress in Homeric Greece are examined with many
parallels made to modern Greece. Illustrated
with drawings and plates.

269 Marketos, Babes I.
1945. A PROVERB FOR IT: 1510 GREEK SAYINGS.
New York: New World. 191 pp.

1,510 sayings classified under eight general
headings: 1) Man as an individual, 2) Sense of
proportion, 3) Man's lot, 4) The natural
world, 5) Personal relations, 6) Formal
relations, 7) Man ordering his world/Man's
resources, 8) Miscellaneous. Each section is
subdivided by more specific topics under which
the proverbs are listed. The proverbs are
listed with no context or information on use.
There are indexes of key words and topics as
well as a bibliography of sources consulted.

270 Matthews, Ernest
1949. Merry Greek Tales from Buffalo. NEW YORK
FOLKLORE QUARTERLY 5: 268-275.

Stories about a folk hero named Stratouhotdas
("Priest of the Streets") collected from a
50-year old Greek woman in 1948.

271 Matthews, M.
1969. Greek Contemporary Handweaving. CIBA

REVIEW 2: 3-34.

An examination of weaving in mainland Greece,
Crete, and the Aegean islands by a British
textile lecturer. Discusses patterns and
different styles and methods of weaving.
Illustrated with photographs of women weaving
and spinning.

272 Mavrides, O.
1977. GESUNDHEITSMAGIE IN WEST-THRAKIEN. EIN
BEITRAG ZUR GRIECHISCHEN VOLKSMEDIZIN. Ph.D.
dissertation, Universität Munster, BRD. 196
pp.

This dissertation examines medicinal magic in
western Thrace, covering the healer, methods
and remedies, success of treatment, and
attitudes of specific supplicants, as well as
the community in general.

273 Mavrogordato, John
1955. Modern Greek Folksongs of the Dead.
JOURNAL OF HELLENIC STUDIES. 75: 42-53.

This article examines songs from various parts
of Greece that deal with the dead. Parts of
songs are quoted in both Greek and English
from various published collections of songs.
Subjects of songs include descriptions of
Hades and how souls get to Hades, songs from
the perspective of the soul, and ceremonial
lamentations. The author contends that such
songs show that the Christian Church had
little effect on popular belief.

274 Mavrogordato, John
1956. DIGENES AKRITES. Oxford: Clarendon. 273
pp.

Mavrogordato's very literal translation of

"Digenes Akritas" is produced parallel to
Emile Legrand's Greek text of 1892. The
introduction covers the history and discovery
of the ballad, versions of the story, various
manuscripts, and previous scholarship.

275 Mazarake, Eustathios D.
1959. SYMBOLE STE MELETE TES LAOGRAPHIAS [A
Contribution to the Study of Folklore].
Athens: Estia. 209 pp.

Mazarake states that the purpose of folklore
is the collection, comparison and study of
elements transmitted by oral and written
tradition, and that folklore is concerned with
every area of life and study. This important
book examines the state of folklore research
and areas of folklore study in Europe as known
at the time of publication. Some of the
chapters included cover definition of
folklore, origin and cause, collective memory,
continuity, modification of folkloric
subjects, and disappearance/reappearance of
folkloric subjects. Detailed summaries of
each chapter are provided in English and
French, as well as a lengthy bibliography.

276 Mazarake, Eustathios D.
1964. E LAOGRAPHIKE EREVNA KAI E SYSTEMATIKE
ORGANOSE TIS [Folkloric Research and its
Systematic Organization]. Athens: s.n.   213
pp.

In thirteen chapters this book surveys the
state of folklore research around the world,
its importance to a national culture, and ways
of study. The author discusses methods of
research and fieldwork, use and significance
of archives and libraries, and tools such as
the folklore atlas and dictionary. Detailed
chapter summaries in English and French, and a
lengthy bibliography are included.

277 McGrady, Donald
   1970. Some Spanish and Italian Descendants of
   a Medieval Greek Tale (The Scholar and his
   Imaginary Egg). ROMANCE PHILOLOGY 23: 303-305.

   This article describes a medieval Greek
   folktale of which later versions developed in
   other countries.

278 McPherson, Florence
   1889. Historical Notes on Certain Modern Greek
   Folksongs. JOURNAL OF HELLENIC STUDIES 10:
   86-89.

   Notes on three ballads and examination of
   their place in history.

279 Megas, Giorgios A.
   1939-1949. Zetemata Ellenikes Laographias
   [Questions of Greek Folklore]. EPETERIS TOU
   LAOGRAPIKOU ARCHEIOU TES AKADEMIAS ATHENON
   1939: 99-149; 1940: 110-205; 1941-42: 77-195;
   1943-44: 86-144; 1945-49: 3-100.

   Megas, the important Greek folklorist and
   director of the Folklore Archives at the
   Academy of Athens, details areas to be covered
   by persons collecting folkloric materials in
   Greece. The twelve areas are 1) social
   organization, 2) folk law, 3) pregnancy and
   child birth, 4) children's games, 5) marriage,
   6) death, 7) magic and divination, 8)
   divination, 9) astrology, 10) weather, 11)
   popular medicine, 12) folk religion. A useful
   aid for the ethnographer and folklorist.

280 Megas, George A.
   1951. THE GREEK HOUSE: ITS EVOLUTION AND ITS
   RELATION TO THE HOUSES OF THE OTHER BALKAN

PEOPLES. Athens: Ministry of Reconstruction. 134 pp.

This book is divided into three parts: Greek dwellings, houses of Slavic peoples in the Balkans, and dwellings of Albanians. Many photographs and drawings illustrate the work. Appendices include a lengthy bibliography and a diagrammed explanation of the evolution of each type of dwelling.

281 Megas, G.
1955. DER BARTLOSE IM NEUGRIECHISCHEN MARCHEN. FF Communications 64. Helsinki: Suomalainen Tiedakatemia. 16 pp.

This short study focuses on the character of the beardless man as he appears in print and oral folktales from many locations in Greece. He is compared to other beardless characters in literature.

282 Megas, Giorgios A.
1956. HELLENIKA PARAMYTHIA [Greek Folktales]. Athens: s.n. 238 pp.

This book includes text and notes for forty tales in the Athens Folklore Archives: eleven animal stories, twenty-three folktales, six humorous narratives.

283 Megas, Giorgios A.
1955-56. Kallimachou kai Chrysorroes Hypotheses. In MELANGES OFFERTS A OCTAVE ET MELPO MERLIER A L'OCCASION DU 25E ANNIVERSAIRE DE LEUR ARRIVEE EN GRECE, vol.2. 147-172 pp. Athens: L'Institut Français d'Athènes.

Megas analyzes the motifs in the love story of Kallimachos and Chrysorroes. He attempts to distinguish motifs that came from folklore

from those than came from history, then
examines them to see how they were changed by
the poet.

284 Megas, George A.
1958. GREEK CALENDAR CUSTOMS. Athens: Press
and Information Department, Prime Minister's
Office. 159 pp.

This book describes holidays in Greece and the
customs, beliefs, and rituals, etc.,
associated with them. Discussion of holidays
is in calendar order beginning with October 26
(St. Demetrius Day). Variations of
celebrations by region are given and the book
is illustrated with firty-six photographs.
Megas' introduction discusses attitudes about
the supernatural, the Greek church's attempts
to stamp out such attitudes, and the blending
of Christian and pagan beliefs.

285 Megas, Giorgios A.
1958. "Der un sein schones Weiss Beneidete"
Aa.Th.465. HESSISCHE BLATTER FUR VOLKSKUNDE
49/50: 135-150.

This analysis of the story of "The Tortoise
and the Fairy Wife" includes references to
Greek variants in other sources and a map
showing the location of variants.

286 Megas, George A.
1960. Oral Parallels to Aesop. In HUMANIORIA:
ESSAYS IN LITERATURE, FOLKLORE, BIBLIOGRAPHY
HONORING ARCHER TAYLOR ON HIS 70TH BIRTHDAY,
ed.Wayland D.Hand and Gustave O.Arlt.
pp.195-207. Locust Valley, NY: J.J.Augustin.

This essay compares three original Aesop tales
with published versions and similar popular
versions as collected by Megas or other

folklorists. The author concludes that
folktales have been preserved in a more pure
condition in oral tradition than in
literature.

287 Megas, Giorgios A.
1961. Der griechische Märchenraum und der
Katalog der griechischen Märchenvarianten. In
INTERNATIONALER KONGRESS DER
VOLKSERZAHLUNGFORSCHER IN KIEL UND KOPENHAGEN:
VORTRAGE UND REFERATE. Berlin: de Gruyter.
199-205 pp.

In this paper Megas defines Greece as a
distinct folklore region based on the research
of Dawkins and others.

288 Megas, Giorgios A.
1962. HELLENIKA PARAMYTHIA [Greek Folktales].
Athens: Kollaros. 232 pp.

This book is an illustrated collection of
forty-six folktales.

289 Megas, Giorgios A.
1962. HELLENIKA PARAMYTHIA [Greek Folktales].
Athens: s.n. 242 pp.

This book is an illustrated collection of 40
folktales.

290 Megas, George A.
1965. Die Griechische Erzähltradition in der
Byzantinischen Zeit. LAOGRAPHIA 22: 290-299.

This article reviews the storytelling
tradition in Byzantine Greece.

291 Megas, Giorgios A.

1965. GRIECHISCHE VOLKSMARCHEN. Dusseldorf:
Diederich. 330 pp.

An anthology of seventy-four folktales
translated into German (sixteen animal,
forty-eight fairy tales, ten humorous
stories), this book also includes a discussion
of features of the modern Greek folktale. It
is based on Megas' 1962 collections.

292 Megas, Giorgios A.
1967. Laographike Melete: Demosievthise eis
Diaphora Periodika ektos tes "Laographias"
[Folkloric Studies: Published in Different
Periodicals outside of Laographia]. LAOGRAPHIA
25: 1-703.

A collection of thirty-eight articles by
Megas, in the original languages, published in
journals other than LAOGRAPHIA, this issue is
divided into sections: General, Myths,
traditions and folktales, Folksongs, Habits
and customs, and Philological Works.
Bibliographic notes and a resume of life of
the famous Greek folklorist are included.

293 Megas, Giorgios A.
1968. BEGEGNUNG DER VOLKER IM MARCHEN
UNVEROFFENLICHTE QUELLEN. Band III:
Griechenland-Deutschland. Münster: Aschendorf.
225 pp.

This book contains the original Greek texts
and German translations of eight animal
stories, seventeen tales, and five humorous
narratives collected in Greece between
1873-1959.

294 Megas, George A.
1970. FOLKTALES OF GREECE. Translated by Helen
Colaclides. Chicago: University of Chicago

Press. 287 pp.

A collection of seventy-seven folktales
presented under six subject headings: 1)
Animal tales, 2) Wonder tales, 3) Tales of
kindness rewarded and evil punished, 4) Tales
of fate, 5) Jokes, anecdotes and religious
tales, and 6) Legends. There are notes for
each tale with source information. Richard M.
Dorson's Foreword is an essay on the history
of Greek folklore scholarship, in particular,
folktale study, and a discussion of the terms
myth and folktale. Megas' Introduction
includes a discussion of characters in
folktales. A bibliography of works in Greek
and other languages, plus indexes of motifs
and tale-types make this an especially useful
study of Greek folktales.

295 Megas, Giorgios A.
1971. DAS MARCHEN VON AMOR UND PSYCHE IN DER
GRIECHISCHEN VOLKSUBERLIEFERUNG. Athens:
Pragmateai tes Akademias Athenon. 206 pp.

This very comprehensive study of the tale of
Cupid and Psyche includes motif listings,
variant listings, and sub-type listings for
the tale as found in various parts of Greece
as well as the rest of the world.

296 Megas, George A.
1975. Die Legende von den zwei Erzsündern in
der griechischen Volksüberlieferung. FABULA
16: 113-120.

Examination of the tale of the Great Sinners
as found in Greek folk tradition.

297 Megas, George A.
1976. DIE BALLADE VON DER ARTA-BRUCKE: EINE
VERGLEICHENDE UNTERSUCHUNG. Hetaireia

Makedonikon Spoudon. Hidryma Maleton
Chersonesou tou Haimou. Ekdosies, 150.
Thessaloniki: Institute for Balkan Studies.
204 pp.

Megas collected more than 300 Greek versions
of the famous ballad about immuring a woman in
the foundations of a bridge in order to ensure
its ability to stand. In analyzing all
aspects of this tale of human sacrifice he
concluded that the poem is Greek though it has
been found throughout the Balkans. The second
section of the book is criticism of other
works on the poem. German translation of the
texts of variants from many parts of Greece is
included.

298 Megas, George A.
1977. Die Nouvelle vom menschenfressenden
Lehrer. In DEMOLOGIA E FOLKLORE. STUDI IN
MEMORIA DI GUISEPPE COCCHIARA. pp.199-210.
Palermo: S.S. Flaccovio.

In this essay Megas examines the story of the
ogre teacher, with an account of the plot,
number of variations and where in Greece they
were found.

299 Megas, Giorgias A.
1978. TO ELLENIKO PARAMYTHI. ANALYTIKOS
KATALOGOS TYPON KAI PARALLAGON KATA TO SYSTEMA
AARNE-THOMPSON [The Greek Folktale. An
Analytic Catalog of Types and Parallels
according to the Aarne-Thompson System]. FF
Communications 184. Athens: Akademia Athenon.
112 pp.

The 299 animal tales tales listed by
Aarne-Thompson classification in this book are
from the Folklore Archives of the Academy of
Athens. There is a lengthy bibliography and
list of sources of folktales, including a

useful periodicals list. Plans were made for
three other catalogs of folktales but were
never completed due to the death of Megas.

300 Megas, Giorgios A.
    1983. On the Oedipus Myth. In OEDIPUS: A
    FOLKLORE CASEBOOK, ed.Lowell Edmunds and Alan
    Dundes. pp.133-146. New York: Garland.

    This article examines Oedipus-like tales found
    in various parts of Greece and Cyprus. Megas
    challenges Alexander Krappe's ideas on the
    origin of the Oedipus myth and argues that the
    point is that Oedipus receives his fate at
    birth and cannot change it. He compares it
    with myths found in other cultures and shows
    how ethical elements makes Oedipus more than a
    common tale of fortune.

301 Meraklis, Michel
    1965. Une autre Version de la "Persinette."
    LAOGRAPHIA 22: 300-303.

    This brief article discusses the fact that
    there are twenty-two Greek and two
    Serbo-Croatian versions of the folktale
    "Persinette," also known as "Rapunzel."

302 Merlier, Melpo
    1931. TRAGOUDIA TES ROUMELES [Songs of
    Roumely]. Athens: Sideris. 96 pp.

    The author studied Greek folksongs for many
    years. The introduction to this book, in
    Greek and French, describes her first
    findings. The second section is the
    transcription of sixty-six songs in Greek
    collected during a trip to Roumely in central
    Greece.

303 Merlier, Melpo
1935. ESSAI D'UN TABLEAU DU FOLKLORE MUSICALE
GREC. LE SYLLOGOGUE POUR L'ENREGISTREMENT DES
CHANSONS POPULAIRES. Athens: Sideris. 61 pp.

When this booklet was written there were 639
folk melodies on 222 records in the Folklore
Muoic Arohivoo. It inclnded material recorded
after 1922 from both refugees and residents.
A photograph and biography was taken of every
singer and songs were categorized by region
and type. Madame Merlier briefly discusses
geographic definitions, problems presented and
plans for future recordings.

304 Merlier, Melpo
1948. TO ARCHEIO TES MIKRASIATIKES LAOGRAPHIAS
[The Archives of Asia Minor Folklore].
Collection de l'Institut Français d'Athènes,
7. Athens: Ikaros. 56 pp.

In this book Madame Merlier describes how the
Archives of Asia Minor Folklore was founded in
the Folklore Music Archives, and that the
unprecedented national event of 1922 provoked
the study of folklore of the Greek communities
of Asia Minor. Contributors to the Archives,
upcoming studies, and reasons for gathering
and preserving these materials are discussed.

305 Merlier, Melpo
1960. La chanson populaire grecque. Acta
MUSICOLOGICA 32: 68-77.

This important state-of-the art discussion
divides Greek folksongs into two historical
periods: 1830-1914 and 1914-1957. Merlier
describes archives, collecting and
scholarship, and lists key figures with their
contributions. Activities and collections of
various learned societies interested in folk
music are described. She states that the

decline of traditional folk music was caused
by radio which, at the same time developed
radio folklorists.

306 M., O. (Octave Merlier)
1948. Les Archives Musicales de Folklore et le
Centre d'études Microasiatiques (1930-1949).
BULLETIN ANALYTIQUE DE BIBLIOGRAPHIE
HELLENIQUE 9: xxxiii-xliv.

Octave Merlier, an editor of the BULLETIN
ANALYTIQUE DE BIBLIOGRAPHIE D'ETUDES
MICROASIATIQUES, and husband of Melpo Merlier,
describes twenty years of collecting and
studying folklore of refugees from Asia Minor.
He discusses research methods, key figures,
where research was done, how songs were
registered.

307 Michaelides, Solon
1948. THE NEOHELLENIC FOLK-MUSIC. Limassol,
Cyprus: Nicosia Printing Office. 44 pp.

The author classifies Neohellenic folk music
into three groups: folksongs, folkdances, and
dance-songs, and states that Neohellenic music
began with the fall of Constantinople in 1453.
Using forty-two examples, this short book
examines modes and scales, melodic features,
forms and rhythms, folk dances and
instruments. A list of published folksong
collections is also included.

308 Michaelides, Solon
1949. Greek Folk Music: Its Preservation and
Traditional Practices. JOURNAL OF THE
INTERNATIONAL FOLK MUSIC COUNCIL 1: 21-24.

On the survival and importance of folk music
to rural people, and the physical, racial and
historical factors that help people preserve

folk music, this article is actually a
proposal for folk music study.

309 Michaelides, Solon
    1956. Greek Song-Dances. JOURNAL OF THE
    INTERNATIONAL FOLK MUSIC COUNCIL 8:37-39.

    Description and development of a few
    folkdances.

310 Michaelides, Solon
    1966. The Neohellenic Folk-music: An
    Introduction to its Character. In VOLKSMUSIK
    SUDOSTEUROPAS, ed.Walther Wünsch. pp.153-164.
    Munich: Trofenik.

    The author sees Neohellenic Folkmusic as
    beginning in 1453 with the fall of
    Constantinople and classifies it into three
    groups: folksongs, folkdances and
    dance-songs. Traits from antiquity are found
    in modern songs. Modes and scales, melodic
    features, forms and rhythms, folkdances and
    popular instruments are discussed briefly.

311 Mills, A.Raymond
    1948. Peasant Remedies from the Greek Islands.
    BULLETIN OF THE HISTORY OF MEDICINE 22:
    441-450.

    The author collected remedies in the Aegean
    Islands from 1945-1947 while in the British
    army and in charge of a hospital. Included is
    a glossary of remedies for conditions from
    abortion to wounds, as well as contents,
    mixtures, directions and applications.

312 Mirasyezis, Maria D.
    1975. Les Choix des époux d'après la chanson
    populaire grecque (9e-19e siècles). In ACTES
    DU COLLOQUE INTERNATIONAL, AMOUR ET MARIAGE EN

EUROPE. pp.249-257. Liege: Musée de la Vie
Wallone.

The author states that folksongs reveal much
detail about everyday life. This article
specifically examines three aspects of
choosing one's mate as seen in numerous Greek
folksongs: preferences of a young man,
preferences of a young woman, and the role of
the parents. In finding frequent recurrence
of such traits as physical qualities, money,
love, ability to work, etc., Mirasyezis
concludes that some criteria are timeless and
others influenced by the times.

313 Mistakidou, Aekaterini
1978. COMPARISON OF THE TURKISH AND GREEK
SHADOW THEATER. Ph.D. dissertation, New York
University. 261 pp. DAI 39/06-A p.3232.
Order number 78-24254.

This examination of the shadow theater assumes
that, as folk art, it has developed into a
national individual expression in each
country. The purpose is to study the function
of the plays in relation to the lives of the
Turks and the Greeks. Plays found in both
Greece and Turkey are studied and some are
examined in detail.

314 Molho, Michael
1950. USOS Y COSTUMBRES DE LOS SEFARDIES DE
SALONICA. Madrid: Instituto Arias Montano. 341
pp.

This book on the now-gone Sephardic community
of Thessalonike, includes description of many
customs and beliefs.

315 Morgan, Gareth
1960. Cretan Poetry: Sources and Inspiration:

chapter 1, "The Folksongs," chapter 2, "Digenes in Crete." KRETIKA CHRONIKA [Cretan Chronicles] 14: 7-68.

These are two chapters from Morgan's work on Cretan poetry from 1453-1500 which is published in its entirety throughout this volume of KRETIKA CHRONIKA. Chapter 1 is an attempt to determine what folk poetry existed in Venetian Crete which Morgan does by examining mainly political folk poems in manuscripts, and by comparing them to eighty-four songs in two collections of folk songs compiled in the twentieth century. The second chapter covers the appearance of the important Greek poem "Digenes Akritas" in Crete.

316 Morgan, Gareth
1973. Butz Triads: Towards a Grammar of Folk Poetry. FOLKLORE 94: 44-56.

This article examines and compares triad formula poems from many countries including charms from Skiathos, a curse from Crete, and a love mantinadha.

317 Morgan, Gareth
1973. The Laments of Mani. FOLKLORE 84: 265-298.

The funeral lament is the folk poetry of the Mani region of Greece. This article discusses the subjects of laments, the lament event and types of laments. Many laments show that vendettas were a way of life in Mani society. English translations of twenty-five laments, most from the 1800s, are included. A bibliography of materials (mainly in Greek) on Mani and laments of Mani supplements the article.

318 Mundy, C.S.
1965. Philogelos, the Nesnas, and Misokalakis.
LAOGRAPHIA 22: 324-327.

This article outlines the evolution of Greek
numskull tales from ancient Greece to the
nineteenth century and the influence of
neighboring peoples on the tales.

319 Myers, John L.
1950. Easter in a Greek Village. FOLKLORE 61:
203-208.

A first-hand account of an Easter festival in
a Greek village in northern Euboea in 1893,
this article also includes a description of
Easter in the Dodecanese and 1916 during World
War I, and a discussion of Greek and Easter
customs. The author refers to descriptions of
Greek Easter in travel logs.

320 Myrsiades, Linda S.
1976. The Karaghiozis Performance in
Nineteenth-Century Greece. BYZANTINE AND
MODERN GREEK STUDIES 2: 83-97.

This article surveys the development of the
Karaghiozis play and the history of its
performance. This play was very popular
because it incorporated folktales, costumes,
language and characters that were familiar to
common people of the nineteenth century.

321 Myrsiades, Linda Suny
1980. The Female Role in the Karaghiozis
Performance. SOUTHERN FOLKLORE QUARTERLY 44:
145-163.

The Karaghiozis shadow puppet theater reflects
life in 19th century Greece. This article
discusses the disproportionate balance of male

and female characters, the depiction of women, and what they represent. With the urbanization of shadow theater and Greek life in general, the female characters gained more freedom in their roles. Some dialogues from plays are included.

322 Myrsiades, Linda Suny
1980. Oral Composition and the Karaghiozis Performance. THEATRE RESEARCH INTERNATIONAL 5: 107-121.

The author studied 200 printed texts, recordings, tapes, synopses, and performances of Karaghiozis plays. Originally Turkish, these shadow plays developed their own Greek identity and became entertainment for the urban lower class. Myrsiades finds, in examining stock narrative scenes played by standard characters, that the Karaghiozis performance is part of a larger oral tradition that includes Homeric epics, the Akritic cycle and klephtic ballads. Texts of scenes are included.

323 Nemas, Theodoros A.
1981-83. DEMOTIKA TRAGOUDIA TES THESSALIAS [Popular Songs of Thessaly]. Thessalonike: Kyriakides. 2 vols. 250 pp., 542 pp.

The texts of more than 1,000 songs from the region of Thessaly, found in collections in the Folklore Archives of the University of Thessalonike and from the author's archives, are provided in these two volumes. Arrangement is by type of song which includes Akritic, narrative, historical, Klephtic, lullabies, wedding, pastoral, work, satirical, and moirologhia.

324 Negris, Alexander

1834. A DICTIONARY OF MODERN GREEK PROVERBS.
Edinburgh: Thomas Clark. 144 pp.

This dictionary includes 950 Greek proverbs
translated into English with commentary.

325 Nichols, Priscilla
    1953. Greek Lore from Syracuse, N.Y. NEW YORK
    FOLK QUARTERLY 9: 109-117.

    Describes customs concerned with sickness,
    death, birth, the evil eye, weddings and
    holidays as told to the author by a
    Greek-American couple in Syracuse.

326 Nilsson, Martin
    1961. GREEK FOLK RELIGION. Philadelphia:
    University of Pennsylvania Press. 166 pp.
    (Original: Greek Popular Religion. New York:
    Columbia University Press, 1961.)

    Actually a collection of lectures given in
    1933-40, this book mainly focuses on ancient
    folk religion. Beliefs and rituals that exist
    in modern times are discussed if they are
    related to or seem to have evolved from
    antiquity.

327 Notopoulos, John A.
    1952. Homer and Cretan Heroic Poetry: A Study
    in Comparative Oral Poetry. AMERICAN JOURNAL
    OF PHILOLOGY 73: 225-250.

    The thesis of this article is that the study
    of modern oral poetry sheds light on Homeric
    poetry in three areas: 1) the oral poet and
    composition and recitation, 2) the influence
    of the audience on oral creation, and 3) the
    poet's relation to his material. "The Song of
    Daskaloyannes," a poem sung in Crete is
    studied, with Greek text and English
    translation.

328 Notopoulos, James A.
1957-58. TRAGOUDIA DODEKANESION TES AMARIKES
[Folksongs of the Dodecanese in America].
Laographia 17: 22-29.

This article, which is written in Greek,
discusses folksongs collected in America from
old Greek immigrants from the Dodecanese
islands. Includes text of three songs in
Greek.

329 Nutt, (Miss)_____.
1894. Modern Greek Birth-Customs. FOLKLORE 5:
338-339.

The author describes customs related to
childbirth as told to her by a Greek woman in
Salonica.

330 Oeconomides. D.B.
1956-57. O Dionysus kai e Ampelos en Naxo kata
tas Archaias kai Neoteras Paradoseis [Dionysus
and the Vineyard in Naxos, according to
Ancient and Younger Traditions]. In MELANGES
OFFERTS A OCTAVE ET MELPO MERLIER A L'OCCASION
DU 25E ANNIVERSAIRE DE LEUR ARRIVEE EN GRECE,
vol.2: pp.185-203. Athens: L'Institut
Français d'Athènes.

This article reports on sources from antiquity
and early Christianity, as well as stories and
customs from Naxos and other places related to
viticulture and wine, which deal with the
legend of Dionysus and the vineyard.

331 Oeconomides, Demetrios B.
1965. Yello dans les Traditions des Peuples
Hellenique et Roumain. LAOGRAPHIA 22: 328-334.

This article studies the infant-killer demon "Yello," who appears in folk tradition in many regions of Greece.

332 Orso, Ethelyn
1979. MODERN GREEK HUMOR: A COLLECTION OF JOKES AND RIBALD TALES. Bloomington: Indiana University Press. 262 pp.

During the period of June 1956 to May 1977, the author drove around Greece collecting "funny stories." She went to Pireus, Athens, northern and western cities, Crete, Mykonos, and other islands. She collected jokes from groups, not individuals, using methods associated with participant observation. The importance of humor to Greek life is discussed in the preface and introduction. 346 jokes are published in nine chapters: 1) political jokes, 2) the Bobos jokes, 3) the clever Greeks: esoteric humor, 4) ethnic slur jokes: Greek exoteric humor, 5) humor directed at church and clergy, 6) transportation jokes, 7) lunatic jokes, 8) very sokin (dirty) jokes, 9) light sokin jokes. Tale types and motif numbers are listed with each joke. There are indexes of tale types and motifs, illustrations of gestures used when telling jokes, a glossary and a bibliography.

333 Pachtikos, Giorgios D.
1905. 260 DEMOTHE ELLENIKA ASMATA [260 Greek Folksongs]. Athens: Sakellariou. 410 pp.

This book includes 260 songs collected from Greeks in Asia Minor, Thrace, Macedonia and Crete, as well as mainland Greece and the island. Both text and music are provided.

334 Papadakis, Nikos

1971. GREEK FOLK SILVER VOTIVE OFFERINGS:
ICONOGRAPHICAL CITATION FROM THE ANONYMOUS ART
OF THE GREEK PEOPLE. Translated by Ek.Tsiakma.
Athens: s.n. 119 pp.

This book traces the history of votive
offerings and vows in antiquity, Christianity,
and legends, and describes the significance of
different kinds of silver offerings. The
sixty-eight photographs of votive offerings
are described but without place of origin or
use. The author's stated purpose in writing
this book is to encourage scholarly research
in the area of anonymous votive art.

335 Papamichael, Anna J.
1975. BIRTH AND PLANT SYMBOLISM: SYMBOLIC AND
MAGICAL USES OF PLANTS IN CONNECTION WITH
BIRTH IN MODERN GREECE. Athens: Anna J.
Papamichael. 372 pp.

An exhaustive examination of symbolic and
magical uses of plants that are used in
conception and childbirth. Contemporary use
of plants is compared with earlier uses as
seen in classical and Hellenistic literature,
as well as non-Greek uses. Mythological and
religious origins are explored. Functions
covered are begetting of children, procreation
of male offspring, causes of sterility, and
easy labor and delivery. Maps, figures and 93
plates of plants illustrate the book. There
is extensive documentation, a list of sources,
a bibliography, Greek and English indexes, and
an index of motifs, images and properties of
plants.

336 Papanikolas, Helen Zeese
1970. Magerou: The Greek Midwife. UTAH
HISTORICAL QUARTERLY 38: 50-60.

This story of a woman who was a midwife in

Greece and continued her role when she came to
a mining town in Utah in 1909 was collected
from Magerou's daughters. She became a folk
doctor and was important to her community and
in interacting with non-Greek doctors.

337 Papanikolas, Helen Zeese
1970. Toil and Rage in a New Land: The Greek
Immigrants in Utah. UTAH HISTORICAL QUARTERLY
38: 98-204.

Using historical records, newspapers and
interviews the author documents immigration of
Greeks to Utah in the early 1900s. Labor
problems are the focus of this study but the
daily life of the people is shown in detail.
Weddings, funerals, holidays and foods are
described. Translations of some folksongs are
included as well as many photographs.

338 Papanikolas, Helen Zeese
1971. Greek Folklore of Carbon County. In LORE
OF FAITH AND FOLLY, ed.T.E.Cheney, assisted by
Austin E.Fife and Juanita Brooks. pp.61-77.
Salt Lake City: University of Utah Press.

A brief discussion of customs, medical
practices, rites of passage and beliefs of the
Cretan and Roumeliot settlers of Carbon
County, Utah, who came to mine coal in the
early 1900's.

339 Papanikolas, Zeese
1982. BURIED UNSUNG: LOUIS TIKAS AND THE
LUDLOW MASSACRE. Salt Lake City: University of
Utah Pr. 332 pp.

This book describes the life and death of a
Greek immigrant labor hero. Written by a man
who is an academic and a third-generation
Greek-American, it is of interest to

folklorists because it shows both the process
of becoming a folk hero and the richness of
oral tradition in Greek folk culture.

340 Papantoniou, Ioanna
    1981. GREEK COSTUMES. Nafplion: Peloponnesian
    Folklore Foundation. 55 pp.

    The introduction provides a short general
    description of women's and men's traditional
    costumes, especially the outer garments.
    Twenty pages each are devoted to color
    photographs of women's and men's costumes with
    brief descriptions. Most of the costumes
    shown here crystalized in the 1800's with
    parts from Medieval and Byzantine times.

341 Paraskevopoulou, Maria
    1978. RECHERCHES SUR LES TRADITIONS DES FETES
    RELIGIEUSES POPULARIES DE CHYPRE. Nicosia,
    Cyprus: Cosmos Pr. 264 pp. (Original: Ph.D.
    dissertation, University of Paris, 1972.)

    Based on the author's dissertation, this book
    looks at religious practices of Cyprus from
    the perspective of folklore, psychology, and
    history of religion. The first section
    describes in detail the Twelve Days (Christmas
    to Epiphany), Carnival, Easter, and
    Kataklysmos. Historical background for each
    festival/holiday is provided. Interpretation
    shows these religious celebrations to be
    survivals from antiquity. The second part is
    on the cults of saints and the Virgin. A
    calendar of saints' days is included with
    explanation of significance and appropriate
    behavior. Most data come from printed
    sources, some from interviews. Approximately
    seventy-five leaves of plate of color
    photographs of icons, churches, religious
    bread, and people participating in festivals
    are included.

342 Passow, Arnold
    1860. POPULARIA CARMINA GRAECIAE RECENTORIS.
    Leipzig: Teubner. 650 pp.

    This book contains 646 songs and 1157 distichs
    with critical discussion for each song. Most
    of the items here were taken from previously
    published sources although some were collected
    by the author.

343 Paton, W.R.
    1890. Gunaikeia from the Greek island of
    Calymnos. FOLKLORE 1: 523-524.

    This short article on women's folklore
    describes customs related to pregnancy, birth,
    menstruation and marriage.

344 Paton, W.R.
    1895. St. John's Eve in the Greek Islands.
    FOLKLORE 6: 94,199.

    Customs for St. John's Eve as seen by the
    author and his wife on the island of Calymnos.

345 Paton, W.R.
    1899-1901. Folktales from the Greek Islands.
    FOLKLORE 10: 495-502; 11: 113-119, 333-344,
    452-456; 12: 84-97, 197-208, 317-325.

    This series of articles provides the text of
    twenty-five folktales collected by the author
    in Lesbos and Calymnos. Names, ages, and
    descriptive information about the informants
    are included.

346 Paton, W.R.
    1907. Folk-Medicine, Nursery Lore, etc. from

the Aegean Islands. FOLKLORE 18: 329-33.

This article includes various beliefs and folk cures from Kos and Kephalos.

347 Patterson, G.James
1976. THE GREEKS OF VANCOUVER: A STUDY IN THE PRESERVATION OF ETHNICITY. Ottawa: National Museum of Canada. 162 pp.

A study of ethnicity among the 6,000 Greek-Canadians in the Kitsilano area of Vancouver, British Columbia, based on fieldwork done in 1975. The first chapters cover the history of Greek immigration to North America, Greeks in Vancouver, and the Greek community including schools, church, the kafenion and social events. Aspects of community life that bind the community are discussed and include food, medical problems, folk beliefs and folktales, dancing, music, language, and material culture. Thirteen interviews provide life histories of members of the communities. The final chapter discusses the cohesiveness of this Greek-Canadian community as compared with other Greek-American communities. Ilustrated with photographs.

348 Pernot, Hubert
1903. MELODIES POPULAIRES GRECQUES DE L'ILE DE CHIO. Paris: Imprimerie nationale. 129 pp.

Pernot is reputed to be the first person to record Greek folksongs. This includes 114 songs translated into French with music.

349 Pernot, Hubert
1903. Rapport sur une mission scientifique en turquie. NOUVELLES ARCHIVES DES MISSIONS SCIENTIFIQUES ET LITTERAIRES 11: 116-241.

In this report Pernot describes his linguistic mission of 1898 and 1899 to collect and record songs on the island of Chios. He provides scores for 114 songs which include baptismal songs, lullabies, marriage songs, work songs, and moirologhia. The name, age, and occupation of the singer and the town where it was recorded is given for each song. When they exist versions of a song are included. The introduction is in French.

350 Petrides, Theodore and Elfleida Petrides
     1974. FOLK DANCES OF THE GREEKS: ORIGINS AND INSTRUCTIONS. Folkestone: Bailey Brothers and Swinfen. 79 pp.

     This book describes many Greek dances and provides some history and lore surrounding each. Instructions for steps, as well as diagrams for feet and regional variations, are given for each dance.

351 Petrides, Ted
     1975. GREEK DANCES. Athens: Lycabettus Press. 103 pp.

     An instruction manual for eighteen dances: five from Crete and thirteen from other islands and the mainland. For each dance there is a brief introduction with history and customs and instructions with feet diagrams.

352 Petrides, Ted
     1976. GREEK DANCES AND HOW TO DO THEM. Athens: Lycabettus Press. 167 pp.

     An instruction manual for twenty-five dances. Each set of instructions has feet diagrams and a brief history on the particular dance. Illustrated with photographs.

353 Petropoulos, Demetrios A.
1951. La contribution française au développement
de la science du folklore en Grèce. BULLETIN.
ASSOCIATION GUILLAUME BUDE, ser.3, no.2:
85-98.

This article describes contributions of French
scholars to the study of Greek folklore.
Petropoulos considers France to be the first
country interested in modern Greece, beginning
with Fauriel's publication of Greek folksongs
in 1824-25 and the founding of l'Ecole
Française d'Athènes, a research institute, in
1846.

354 Petropoulos, Demetrios A.
1952. The Study of Ethnography in Greece.
MIDWEST FOLKLORE 2: 15-20.

This article surveys the history and status of
ethnographic studies in Greece, including
folklore and music. Includes information on
the founding of societies, journals and
archives.

355 Petropoulos, Demetrios A.
1954. LA COMPARISON DANS LA CHANSON POPULAIRE
GRECQUE. Collection de l'Institut Français
d'Athènes, 86. Athens: L'Institut Français
d'Athènes. 168 pp.

This work discusses similie, metaphor and
allegory, and their roles in modern Greek oral
poetry from Byzantine times to the present. A
lengthy bibliography is included.

356 Petropoulos, Demetrios A.
1955. Survivances de Sacrifices d'Animaux en
Grèce. In PAPERS OF THE INTERNATIONAL CONGRESS

OF EUROPEAN AND WESTERN ETHNOLOGY, STOCKHOLM,
1951. pp.120-125. Stockholm: International
Commission of Folk Arts and Folklore and the
Swedish Organizing Committee of the Congress.

The author describes and briefly interprets
animal sacrifices in Greece, in particular
those connected with the Anastenaria. Other
works on this subject by Greek folklorists are
discussed as well as the practice of sacrifice
in the Old Testament.

357 Petropoulos, Demtrios
    1956-57. Le rôle des Femmes et de la Terre en
    quelques Pratiques Magiques. In MELANGES
    OFFERTS A OCTAVE ET MELPO MERLIER A L'OCCASION
    DU 25E ANNIVERSAIRE DE LEUR ARRIVEE EN GRECE,
    vol.2. 275-285 pp. Athens: L'Institut
    Français d'Athènes.

    This article examines the customs and beliefs
    about rebirth and the history behind them.

358 Petropoulos, Demetrios A.
    1965. Das Rampsinitos-Märchen in
    Neugriechischen Uberlieferungen. LAOGRAPHIA
    22: 43-53.

    This study of a very old story in modern Greek
    storytelling tradition focuses on the mythic
    king Rampsinitos, first recorded in Herodotus.
    The article discusses origins and version and
    includes a Pontic version of the story
    collected in 1918.

359 Petropoulos, Elias
    1979. REBETIKA TRAGOUDIA. Athens: Kedros. 709
    pp.

    This encyclopedia of rebetika, a type of Greek
    underground music, includes lyrics to more

than 1000 songs, many of them collected by the
author from prisoners while himself in
prison. It also includes a photographic
history of rebetika and articles by other
writers on rebetic music.

360 Pio, Jean
     1879. NEOELLENIKA PARAMYTHIA. CONTES
     POPULAIRES GRECS. Copenhagen: Høst. 260 pp.

     This collection of forty-seven tales in Greek
     was published from the manuscripts of Johann
     Georg von Hahn. Tales are from Epiros,
     Astypalaias, Tinos and Syros, and are in Greek
     with notes.

361 Politis, Nikolaos G.
     1871-74. MELETE EPI TOU NEOTERON ELLENON:
     NEOELLENIKE MYTHOLOGIA [Studies on the Life of
     Modern Greeks: Modern Greek Mythology].
     Athens: Wilberg and Nake. 2 vols. 527 pp.

     This collection of tales covers the universe,
     nature, Olympic gods, worldly divinities or
     demons, Fate, the Underworld, and giants.

362 Politis, N.G.
     1894. On the Breaking of Vessels as a Funeral
     Rite in Modern Greece. JOURNAL OF THE
     ANTHROPOLOGICAL INSTITUTE OF GREAT BRITAIN AND
     IRELAND 23: 29-41.

     Description of funeral practices in different
     parts of Greece, in particular the breaking of
     vessels, throwing earth on the coffin, and
     sprinkling water on the ground. Describes and
     examines the functions of such rites.

363 Politis, Nikolaos G.
     1899-1902. MELETAI PERI TOU BIO KAI TES

GLOSSES TOU HELLENIKOU LAOU: PAROIMIAI
[Studies on the Life and Language of the Greek
Peoples: The Proverbs]. Athens: Sakellarios. 4
vols. 600 pp., 699 pp., 686 pp., 686 pp.

This major work lists proverbs alphabetically
by key-word with sources and commentary.
Unfortunately, it only gets to the fifth
letter of the alphabet. Volume 1 includes
bibliographies of Greek proverb collections
and proverb studies in other countries.

364 Politis, Nikolaos G.
    1904. MELETAI PERI TOU BIOU KAI TES GLOSSES
    TOU HELLENIKOU LAOU: PARADOSEIS [Studies on
    the Life and Language of the Greek People: The
    Legends]. Athens: Sakellariou. 2 vols. 1348
    pp.

A collection of all Greek legends known up to
1904, Vol.A provides text with place of origin
and Vol.B has commentary on each tale.
Legends are arranged in general and sub-areas,
including Historical, Royalty, Ancient
Hellenes, Ancient gods and heroes,
Christianity, Supernatural, and Magic.

365 Politis, Nikolaos G.
    1909. Laographia [Folklore]. LAOGRAPHIA 1:
    3-18.

In this seminal article, the father of Greek
folklore defines laographia and sets down the
organization of materials for folklore
research. He emphasizes the importance of
transcribing oral tradition and describing
traditional acts, and subdivides these broad
areas into ten and twenty sub-areas,
respectively.(See Herzfeld, 1982, for a
summary of the scheme in English.)

366 Politis, Nikolaos G.

1914. EKLOGE APO TA TRAGOUDIA TOU ELLENIKOU
LAOU [Selections from the Songs of the Greek
People]. Athens: Estia. 304 pp.

This work is a thorough examination of some
selected ballads, including historical and
linguistic notes, as well as sources and
variants of each ballad. The first
classification of Greek folksongs is found
here, which was used by other scholars,
particularly Stilpon Kyriakides.

367 Politis, Nikolaos G.
1920-31. LAOGRAPHIKA SYMMETIKA [Various
Studies on Folklore]. Athens: Grapheiou
Demosievmeton Akademias Athenon. 3 vols. 304
pp., 470 pp., 393 pp.

This set is a three-volume republication of
various articles by Politis. Vol.1 includes
the author's most popular publications. Vol.2
includes less well-known articles, some of
which are rewritten with new observations.
Vol.3 is special studies.

368 Politis, Y.N.
1886. Local Greek Myths. FOLKLORE JOURNAL 4:
250-252.

Two local myths are recounted here: one about
the Stringlas (supernatural witches) from a
village in the Pelopennesus, the other from
Attica about a cursed islet.

369 Puchner, Walter
1976. Spuren frauenbündischer
Organisationsformen in neugriechischen
Jahreslaufbrauchtum. SCHWEIZERISCHES ARCHIV
FUR VOLKSKUNDE 72: 146-170.

This article describes the involvement of

women in modern Greek calendar customs as found in published sources. Separate sections describe what small girls, big girls, women, and matrons do at the various holidays.

370 Pym, H.
1968. THE SONGS OF GREECE. London: Sunday Times. 96 pp.

This illustrated book is a collection of Greek folksongs collected and translated by the author. A list of recordings is included.

371 Ragovin, Frederick
1974. CRETAN MANTINADES: SONG POEMS. Athens: Cnossos Editions. 71 pp.

This article calls mantinadhes, traditional love poems, the most popular form of musical expression on Crete. From the thousands the author has collected, 300 of the most common mantinadhes are presented here in nineteen subject categories, with Greek and English translation. The introduction briefly describes occasions where they are sung, how they are sung and appropriate musical instruments for accompaniment.

372 Ratliff, Neil
1974. Modern Greek Folk Music and Dance in the New York Public Library. NOTES OF THE MUSIC LIBRARY ASSOCIATION 27: 725-731.

This bibliography lists sixty-nine titles on modern Greek folk music and dance in the Music Division of the New York Public Library. Books, pamphlets issued with recordings, and periodicals are arranged in general and geographical sections. Some works are briefly annotated.

373 Rennell, James Rennell Rodd, Baron
    1892. THE CUSTOMS AND LORE OF MODERN GREECE.
    London: Stott. 198 pp.

    Based on two years of travel through Greece in
    the late nineteenth century, this book
    includes the author's account of festivals,
    marriage, birth, death, beliefs and
    ceremonies, the supernatural, healing, songs
    and poetry.

374 Romaios, C.A.
    1949. CULTES POPULAIRE DE LA THRACE. LES
    ANASTENARIA. LA CEREMONIE DU LUNDI PUR.
    Collection de l'Institute Français d'Athènes,
    18. Athens: L'Institut Français d"Athènes.
    213 pp.

    This book is two separate studies based on
    earlier printed sources and is the author's
    attempt to find the origins of the Anastenaria
    and Pure Monday. For each ritual, the author
    describes the ceremony as seen in various
    northern Greek villages, makes an
    interpretation and conclusion, and provides a
    bibliography.

375 Romaios, C.A.
    1954. Les Anasténaria. L'HELLENISME
    CONTEMPORAIN, ser.2, 8: 227-237.

    This article is actually a synopsis of a study
    of the Anastenaria from the author's 1949 book
    on Thracian cults. Portions of the book are
    quoted verbatim.

376 Rouse, W.H.D.
    1905. Presidential Address. FOLKLORE 16:
    14-26.

In this lecture the author recommends Greece
and Slavic countries as rich in folklore.
They offer to the folklorist continuity from
antiquity. He cites examples of beliefs,
behavior, and folktales as survivals.

377 Rouse, W.H.D.
    1896. Folklore First Fruits from Lesbos.
    FOLKLORE 7: 142-159.

    Collected folklore of Lesbos, including
    charms, calendar customs, cures, and local
    holy sites. Illustrated with photographs.

378 Rouse, W.H.D.
    1899. Folklore from the Southern Sporades.
    FOLKORE 10: 150-185.

    The author believed this work to be the first
    published collection of materials from the
    island of Kos. The manners and customs, texts
    of magical charms, calendar customs, beliefs
    in the supernatural, and text of the poem,
    "The Bridge of Antimachia," published here are
    mainly from the Jacob Zarraftis manuscripts.

379 Roussel, Louis
    1921. KARAGHEUZ, OU UN THEATRE D'OMBRES A
    ATHENES. Athens: Raftanis. 2 vols. 52 pp., 60
    pp.

    This study of the Karaghiozis shadow theater
    includes summaries in French of 28 plays.

380 Roussel, Louis
    1929. CONTES DE MYCONO. Léopol: Société
    savante des sciences et des lettres. 441 pp.

    This book includes the phonetic translation of
    eighty-four tales from Myknonos with French

translation.

381 Safilios-Rothschild, Constantina
1965. Morality, Courtship and Love in Greek
Folklore. SOUTHERN FOLKLORE QUARTERLY 29:
297-308.

Examines philotimo--love of honor--and shame
in folksongs, folktales and proverbs. The
author finds that the values expressed are
norms among rural Greeks.

382 Sakellariou, Chares
1940. GREEK DANCES. ELLENIKE CHORE. Athens:
s.n. 122 pp.

Fifty dances arranged for song and piano in
Greek. Text of twenty dances in Greek and
English. Some notes in English.

383 Sanders, Irwin T.
1962. RAINBOW IN THE ROCK: THE PEOPLE OF RURAL
GREECE. Cambridge: Harvard University Press.
363 pp.

This comprehensive description of Greek rural
life is based on fieldwork done in 1952-53. A
sociological study, it includes descriptions
of marriage, childbirth, holy days, and
ceremonies with texts of interviews included.

384 Saunier, Guy
1979. "ADIKIA": LE MAL ET L'INJUSTICE DANS LES
CHANSONS POPULARIES GRECQUES. Paris: Les
Belles Lettres. 398 pp.

This study of the concept of evil as expressed
in folk songs and its relationship to the
metaphysical and moral attitudes of the Greek
people, is based on study of songs in

published works and in manuscripts of the
Folklore Archives of the Academy of Athens.
The author defines terms of evil, justice and
the just, examines the idea of evil in Greek
society and family, and discusses
representations of death in moirologhia,
distichs, songs of Charos, and other
folksongs.

385 Schmidt, Bernhard
1871. DAS VOLKSLEBEN DER NEUGRIECHEN UND DAS
HELLENISCHE ALTERTUM. Leipzig: Teubner. 252
pp.

Schmidt was a German scholar who rallied to
the Greek side after the Fallmerayer
accusations. In this classic work he studies
manners and customs which he observed in the
Ionian islands, as well as the mainland, in
order to show survivals from antiquity.

386 Schmidt, Bernhard
1877. GRIECHISCHE MARCHEN, SAGEN UND
VOLKSLIEDER. Leipzig: Teubner. 285 pp.
(reprinted Hildesheim: G.Olms, 1978.)

This book contains twenty-five folktales,
fourteen legends and seventy songs in Greek
and in German which were collected in Zante.

387 Schmidt, Bernhard
1913. Das böse Blick und Ahnlicher Zauber in
Neugriechischen Volksglauben. NEUE JAHRBUCHER
FUR DAS KLASSISCHE ALTERTUM GESCHICTE UND
DEUTSCHE LITERATURE 31: 574-613.

This article is a very comprehensive study of
all aspects of the evil eye in Greece,
including cause, methods of prevention, and
cures. Many of the examples cited are from
Zante where they were collected by Schmidt.

388 Sike, Yvonne de and Muriel Hutter
1973. Le Chant du destin: Quelques aspects de
la conception de la mort en Grèce à travers
les miriologues. In LES HOMMES ET LA MORT:
RITUELS FUNERAIRES A TRAVERS LE MONDE, ed.Jean
Guiart. pp.59-71. Paris: Muséum national
d'histoire naturelle.

This essay studies the way death is seen in
the moirologhia, which are songs of destiny,
songs of Charon, and the funeral laments for a
specific individual. Death is perceived as a
drama. The songs, as well as some of the
rituals that accompany their singing, are
described, and the French translation of many
songs is included. Mainly based on author's
analysis of songs published collections.

389 Simon, Andrea Judith
1977. THE SECRET SECT AND THE SECULAR CHURCH:
SYMBOLS OF ETHNICITY IN ASTORIA'S GREEK
COMMUNITY. Ph.D dissertation, City University
of New York. 248 pp. DAI 38/04-A p.2221.
Order number 77-20521.

This study compares two Greek Orthodox
churches in New York in order to examine the
effect of social class on symbolic systems
within the context of the church that
influence all aspects of the participants'
lives.

390 Smith, Arnold C.
1962. THE ARCHITECTURE OF CHIOS: SUBSIDIARY
BUILDINGS, IMPLEMENTS AND CRAFTS. ed.Philip
P.Argenti. London: Alec Tiranti. 171 pp.

This book examines all types of Chian
architecture, including religious and
domestic, village homes, and medieval houses.

It is not a comparative study but describes in great detail, and with the aid of maps and 227 plates of drawings, houses, outhouses, orchards, wine presses, village ovens, windmills, household implements, and decoration. This work, which describes how tools are used, rooms laid out, and how some buildings were built, is based on the author's study of Chian architecture in 1936-39.

391 Soyter, Gustav
1921-25. Das volkstümliche Distichon beiden Neugriechen: Ein Beitrage zur Kenntnis der neugriechischen Volksdichtung. LAOGRAPHIA 8: 379-426.

This important study of distichs examines both text and music and has sections on all other aspects including sources, the origin of the word distichon, local dissemination, meaning, meter and rhyme, enunciation, and melody and accompaniment. Text in Greek of many distichs is included.

392 Soyter, Gustav
1939-40. Die neugriechischen Sprichworter in der Volksliedersammlung Werner von Haxthausen. BYZANTINISCH-NEUGRIECHISCHE JAHRBUCHER 16: 171-189.

This article examines eighty-two modern Greek proverbs that originally came from fables. Proverbs are in Greek with German translation.

393 Soyter, Gustav
1961. GRIECHISCHER HUMOR VON ZEITEN BIS HEUTE. Berlin: Akademie Verlag. 157 pp.

This book traces humor from classical times, through Hellenistic and Byzantine periods, to modern Greek humor (i.e. post-War of

Independence). The section on modern Greek
humor includes many examples of satirical
literature and popular literature, including
swallow songs, riddles and puns, and proverbs.

394 Spyridakis, Giorgios
1948. Le folklore en Grece. Chronique
bibliographie pour les années 1940-1947.
BULLETIN ANALYTIQUE DE BULLETIN HELLENIQUE:
i-xxxi.

The author of this review article was an
important folklorist and on the staff of the
Folklore Archives at the Academy of Athens.
Journals for specific regions and islands are
listed. Articles published in major research
journals during 1940-47 as well as important
earlier works are listed and briefly
reviewed. Arrangement is by subject which
includes Byzantine period, modern Greek
folklore, folk habitation, costume, popular
beliefs, theater, folksongs, legends and
tales, proverbs, music and dance, riddles,
rites of passage, and games.

395 Spyridakis, Giogios
1960. The Folklore Archives of the Athens
Academy. JOURNAL OF THE INTERNATIONAL FOLK
MUSIC COUNCIL 12: 75-76.

A description of the Folklore Archives in
1960, Spyridakis describes the holdings of
material collected from every region of Greece
and Greek refugees from Asia Minor and Eastern
Thrace. Text of 60,000 folksongs with
variants, folk music on disc and tape, and
films of folkdances are emphasized.

396 Spyridakis, Giorgios
1962-68. HELLENIKA DEMOTIKA TRAGOUDIA. EKLOGE.
TOM.1 [Greek Folksongs. A Selection. Vol.1].

and HELLENIKA DEMOTIKA TRAGOUDIA. MOUSIKE
EKLOGE. TOM.3 [Greek Folksongs. A Music
Selection. Vol.3]. Demosieumata tou
Laographikou Archeiou, ar.7, 10. Athens:
Akademia Athenon. 517 pp., 437 pp.

This first volume of this work begins with an
introduction to the history of Greek folksong
collections and includes lyrics of more than
200 songs. The first section is on Akritic
songs and written by Spyridakis; the second
essay, on historical songs, is by Giorgios
Megas; klephtic songs are covered by Demetrios
Petrpoulos; narrative songs by Spyridakis and
Petropoulos.
The second volume includes music and text for
all kinds of songs included in volume one as
well as lyrical songs, love songs, wedding
songs, dirges, etc., totaling more than 150
songs. The songs were recorded from the Folk
Music Collection of the Greek Folklore
Research Center. Name of informant, age,
place, year recorded, instrumentalists and
vocalists are provided.
At publication, Tom.2 was in preparation.
This volume is to include indexes for
musicologists and commentary on texts and
music.

397 Spyridakis, Giorgios
     1965. Die alte Frau als Verräterin in einegen
     Neugriechischen Volkssagen. LAOGRAPHIA 22:
     527-530.

     This article discusses a modern Greek version
     of the old tale of a traitorous old woman.

398 Spyridakis, Giorgios
     1967. Situation Universitaire de la
     "Laographie" en Grèce. ETHNOLOGIA EUROPAEA 1:
     277.

An examination of folklore study in Greek universities, including curricula, requirments, archives, research centers, and collections.

399 Spyridakis, Giorgios
1968. Volksliedforschung in Griechenland. JAHRBUCH FUR VOLKSLIEDFORSCHUNG 13: 181-192.

This article surveys the history of academic study of Greek folksongs that began with Europeans, particularly von Haxthausen's 1814 collection of folksongs. The founding of the Folklore Archives with its activities in collecting folksongs was a significant event. Collections of Greek folksongs in German, French, English, and Italian are listed. Spyridakis also lists recent collections of folksongs, recent analytic studies of texts and melodies, studies on folk music, and studies of folk instruments.

400 Stahl, Anca
1976. Animal Sacrifices in the Balkans. In THE REALM OF THE EXTRA-HUMAN: AGENTS AND AUDIENCES, ed.Agehananda Bharati. pp.423-451. The Hague: Mouton.

This article describes animal sacrifices in contemporary Bulgaria, Greece, Romania and Yugoslavia, concentrating on sacrifices for the construction of buildings and sacrifices for the souls of the dead.

401 Stuart-Glennie, J.S.
1892. Greek Folk as Revealed in their Poetry. SCOTTISH REVIEW 32: 113-132.

The author states, "to know a people, one must know its folk-poesy" (p.14). He studies traits and characteristics of the Greek folk by

examining what he sees as the three great
divisions of their poetry: Mythological idylls
and tales, Social songs and stories, and
Historical ballads and legends. He mainly
cites texts included in GREEK FOLK-POESY,
1896, written with Lucy M.J.Garnett.

402 Swanson, Donald
    1960. MODERN GREEK STUDIES IN THE WEST: A
    CRITICAL BIBLIOGRAPHY OF STUDIES ON MODERN
    GREEK LINGUISTICS, PHILOLOGY, AND FOLKLORE IN
    LANGUAGES OTHER THAN GREEK. New York: New York
    Public Library. 93 pp.

    This bibliography lists books and journal
    articles by Greek and western scholars written
    in languages other than Greek. Brief, critical
    annotations as well as citations to book
    reviews are included. The two major sections,
    Books and Monographs, and Periodical Articles,
    are each broken down by four subsections: 1)
    Linguistics, 2) Vulgar Byzantine Texts, 3)
    Modern Popular Literature, and 4) Modern Greek
    Folklore. Section 3 includes works on riddles,
    proverbs, folktales and folksongs, and Section
    4 covers beliefs, customs, festivals, music
    and material culture. A lengthy introduction
    explains the system of selection and
    arrangement.

403 Tarsouli, Athena
    1941. COSTUMES GRECS. Athens: V.
    Papachrysanthou. 12 pp. 65 plates.

    Sixty-five color plates show costumes from the
    regions of Attica, Roumely, Euboea, Thessaly,
    Epirus, Macedonia, and Thrace. The brief text
    of this book is in Greek and French.

404 Tarsouli, Athena
    1951. EMBROIDERIES AND COSTUMES OF THE

DODECANESE. Athens: s.n. 14 pp. 68 plates.

Thirty-one color plates show embroideries of
the Dodecanese and thirty-seven plates show
national costume. The brief text is in Greek
and English and examines influences of other
cultures on Dodecanese costume.

405 Tarsouli, Georgia
    1951. Saint Nicolas dans le folklore grec.
    L'HELLENISME CONTEMPORAIN, ser.2, année 5:
    483-489.

    This article is an historical account of the
    customs, legends and miracles surrounding St.
    Nicholas of Myron from Lycie (Turkey).

406 Tarsouli, Georgia
    1953. Christmas in Greece. MIDWEST FOLKLORE 3:
    231-235.

    A brief description of Christmas customs in
    Greece.

407 Tarsouli, Georgia and Paul G. Brewster
    1959. A Greek Ballad of Near Mother-Son
    Incest. ARV 15: 56-60.

    This article examines thirty-nine variants of
    a Pelopennesian song about a mother's unholy
    love for her son. The theme of mother-son
    incest appears very rarely in balladry.

408 Taylor, John
    1981. The Rebetic Songs. MALEDICTA 5: 10-24.

    This article translates and discusses parts of
    fourteen rebetic songs collected by folklorist
    Elias Petropoulos.

409 Teske, Robert Thomas
1973. The Eikonostasi Among Greek
Philadelphians. PENNSYLVANIA FOLKLIFE 23(1):
20-30.

A study of the use of icons, and beliefs and
attitudes surrounding them, as seen in one
large family. Differences between officially
sanctioned and folk uses of icons are
discussed. Many photographs of icons and icon
arrangements are included.

410 Teske, Robert Thomas
1973. Rules Governing Votive Offerings Among
Greek Philadelphians. KEYSTONE FOLKLORE 18:
181-195.

This article examines the system of making
offerings to saints by studying one
informant's behavior in making a request and
promising a votive offering. To determine
real and ideal behavior the author looked at
the occasion for the vow, the importance of
the occasion, the votant's economic and social
status, and the relationship between the
votant and votive beneficiary. Four
photographs of icons and votive offerings are
included.

411 Teske, Robert Thomas
1977. On the making of Bobonieres and Marturia
in Greek-Philadelphia: Commercialism in Folk
Religion. JOURNAL OF THE FOLKLORE INSTITUTE
14: 151-158.

Bobonieres are sugar-covered almonds in white
netting which are usually distributed at
weddings. Marturia can be figs, coins, or
other things which are given to those who have
witnessed a ceremony. The author studied a
Greek religious goods shop in a Greek-American

Philadelphia community in 1973, and focused on
the acquisition of supplies and production of
these two religious objects. Photographs of a
boboniere and a marturion are included.

412 Teske, Robert Thomas
1979. Living Room Furnishings, Ethnic
Identity, and Acculturation among Greek
Philadelphians. NEW YORK FOLKLORE 5(1-2):
21-31.

This article discusses use by Greek-Americans
of living rooms for ceremonial functions, and
makes comparisons to the saloni in Greece.
Furniture, objets d'art, and color scheme
identify the owners' Greek identity.
Illustrated with photographs, this article is
based on the author's fieldwork among
Greek-Americans in Philadelphia in 1972-74.

413 Teske, Robert Thomas
1980. VOTIVE OFFERINGS AMONG GREEK
PHILADELPHIANS. New York: Arno. 326 pp.
(Original: Ph.D. dissertation, University of
Pennsylvania, 1974.)

Based on fieldwork in one of Philadelphia's
Greek-American communities in 1972-74 and two
months of research in Greece, this
dissertation is an ethnography of votive
practices. Teske interviewed members of the
community on all aspects of the votive
offering and includes many first-person
narratives that deal with requests and vows,
miraculous healings, and making the offering.
The author analyzes the narratives
historically and studies the offerings
symbolically. A survey of scholarship on
votive offerings in Greece and other parts of
Europe is included, as well as photographs of
icons, churches and offerings.

414 Theodoropoulos, Spiro
    1955. Deux originalités de la chanson
    populaire grecque. I. L'idée de la mort. II.
    La manière de chanter des vers. PAPERS OF THE
    INTERNATIONAL CONGRESS OF EUROPEAN AND WESTERN
    ETHNOLOGY, STOCKHOLM, 1951. pp.145-147.
    Stockholm: International Commission on Folk
    Arts and Folklore and the Swedish Organizing
    Committee of the Congress.

    A very brief discussion of two features of the
    Greek folksong: the idea of death, and the
    manner of singing.

415 Theophano, Janet
    1978. Feast Fast and Time. PENNSYLVANIA
    FOLKLIFE 27(3): 25-32.

    This article is based on fieldwork with Greek
    Orthodox Philadelphians in the 1970s and is a
    study of continuity in foodways. The author
    compares food patterns of ancient and modern
    Greeks and Greek-Americans in Philadelphia.
    Included are discussions of life-cycle events
    and food, calendrical rites and food, and
    seasonal food.

416 Theros, Aghia
    1951. La poésie popularie grecque et la
    mort." L'HELLENISME CONTEMPORAIN, ser.2,
    année 5: 225-240.

    In the introduction to this article the author
    outlines the evolving definition of folklore
    in Greece from Politis to Kyriakidis to Megas
    to Romaios. That folklore is more than
    survivals but also involves psychological and
    historical elements is quite apparent in the
    study of moirologhia or lamentations. The
    three types are ancient, with standard
    variants for babies, old men, young men, etc.;

those made up of old and new elements; and
spontaneous moirologhia for heroes, soldiers
and great persons. A funeral in Mani in 1904
is described and the text of sixteen
moirologhia from various parts of Greece with
French translation is included.

417 Thompson, M.S. .
    1908. Notes from Greece and the Aegean. Evil
    Eye Charms. FOLKLORE 19: 469-70.

    This article describes evil eye charms as seen
    in Sparta, Crete and Rhodes in 1908. Includes
    a photograph of charms drawn on houses in
    Rhodes.

418 Thumb, Albert
    1910. HANDBUCH DER NEUGRIECHISCHEN
    VOLKSPRACHE. Strassburg: Trübner. 240 pp.

    This pioneer discussion of modern Greek
    vernacular includes songs, distich, riddles
    and tales.

419 Tilton, Edward L.
    1895. Lenten Ceremony at Pylos in Greece.
    FOLKLORE 6: 205-206.

    This article briefly describes a Lenten ritual
    in Pylos in 1895.

420 Tommaseo, Niccolo and Paulo Emilio Pavolini
    1905. CANTI DEL POPOLO GRECO. Milan: Sandron.
    200 pp. (Original: Canti Popolari, v.3-4.
    Venice: Tasso, 1842.)

    This book is a collection of 159 songs and 188
    distichs translated into Italian by one of the
    first Italian collectors of folksongs.

421 Tozer, H.F.
    1884. Folklore of Modern Greece. ACADEMY 26:
    71-72.

    Actually a book review of E.M.Geldart's
    FOLK-LORE OF MODERN GREECE, this article
    summarizes publications of Greek folktales as
    of 1884.

422 Tozer, Henry F.
    1889. The Greek-Speaking Population of
    Southern Italy. JOURNAL OF HELLENIC STUDIES
    10: 11-42.

    Based on the work of earlier writers as well
    as the author's visits to Italian-Greek
    colonies in 1887 and interviews with a priest
    and a school master from those communities,
    this article discusses songs and proverbs of
    Greek-Italians. In studying religious songs,
    love songs and dirges, Tozer found that the
    songs are unique and different from those
    found in Greece. Text and translation of ten
    songs and eight proverbs are included.

423 Triantaphyllidis, A.
    1948. Christmas Customs and Folklore. HELLENIA
    3(Dec.): 2-4.

    This article describes beliefs about the
    "kallikanzari," demons who appear on earth
    during the twelve days between Christmas Eve
    and Epiphany and annoy people. The origin of
    this belief is unknown and the Church tried in
    vain to suppress it.

424 Vryonis, Speros
    1975. Local History and Folklore from the
    Village of Vasilkadhes, in the District of
    Erissos, Cephallenia. In ESSAYS IN MEMORY OF

BASIL LAOURDAS, pp.397-424. Thessaloniki:
Gregorios.

The customs surrounding the building of new
houses in the author's home village of
Vasilikadhes, Kephalonia, is the subject of
this essay. It is based on legends and local
documents and archives which reveal the social
history of the village.

425 Wace, A.J.B.
1909-10. North Greek Festivals and the Worship
of Dionysus. ANNUAL OF THE BRITISH SCHOOL OF
ATHENS 16: 232-253.

This article describes the Epiphany plays of
the Kalogheros, including stock characters,
costumes, and details of the dramas, as well
as related activities of other festivals as
they occurred in Thessaly. Data on the plays
were collected from participants by the author
in the first decade of the twentieth century.
Illustrated with photographs and includes
eleven songs.

426 Wace, A.J.B.
1912-13. Mumming Plays in the Southern
Balkans. ANNUAL OF THE BRITISH SCHOOL AT
ATHENS 19: 248-265.

In this article Wace describes Greek and Vlach
masquerades or folk dramas as observed in his
travels in Macedonia and Thessaly in
1910-1912. From his own experience and review
of the literature on mumming in the southern
Balkans, he is unable to make any conclusions
as to their origins, other than as possible
descendants of Dionysian rites. Illustrated
with many photographs.

427 Wace, Alan J.B. and M.S.Thompson

1914. THE NOMADS OF THE BALKANS: AN ACCOUNT OF
LIFE AND CUSTOMS AMONG THE VLACHS OF NORTHERN
PINDUS. London: Methuen, 1914.

This first-hand account of Vlach life is
illustrated with many photographs. Includes
texts of songs.

428 Wace, A.J.B.
1935. MEDITERRANEAN AND NEAR EASTERN
EMBROIDERIES FROM THE COLLECTION OF MRS. F.H.
COOK. 2 vols. London: Halton. 88 pp., 135
plates.

This catalog of 120 pieces of embroidery held
in a private collection includes some from
Greece. The author, an authority on Greek
island embroideries, discusses problems of
classification. The first volume is text and
the second volume is plates of the
embroideries.

429 Wagstaff, J.
1965. Traditional Houses in Modern Greece.
GEOGRAPHY 50: 58-64.

Describes and includes drawings of Greek house
types. The author states that improved
communications are destroying traditional
forms of architecture. A map is included
which shows the kinds of roofs used in
different parts of Greece.

430 Walker, Mrs.W.A.
Some Greek Folklore. FOLKLORE JOURNAL 1:
217-220.

The author records many miscellaneous
superstitions she observed while living in
Greece.

431 Williams, Neil Wynn
1892. A Wedding and a Christening in Greece.
GENTLEMAN'S MAGAZINE 273: 338-349.

The author describes a wedding he observed in
detail, including clothing, ritual behavior,
etc. A christening in Euboea in 1890 is also
described.

432 Zakhos, Emmanuel
1966. POESIE POPULARIE DES GRECS. Paris:
Maspero. 231 pp.

A collection of seventy-four poems, mainly
folk poems, in Greek and French, taken from
published sources or collected by the author.
The poems are arrange by broad subject: 1)
Mountains, 2) Plains, 3) Intergroups, 4)
Ottoman cities, and 5) Modern cities. The
introduction is a lengthy essay on the various
kinds of poems.

433 Zinanovic, Srboljub
1976. The Origin of the Saint's Feast in
Macedonia. MAN 11: 595-596.

This letter discusses the origin of a festival
of the Slavs of Greek Macedonia which shows
the conversion of Slavic tribes by Greek
Christians.

SUBJECT INDEX

(NB: "Collectanea" indexes entries, usually older works, which describe or include a melange of behaviors and/or genres, including beliefs, customs, charms, folktales, folksongs, legends, etc. The term "Collections and archives" refers to works which discuss collections or archives, as well as works which use a significant amount of material from a specific collection.)

Amulets: See Charms
Anastenaria 011, 018, 049, 063, 064, 077, 080, 119, 203, 356, 374, 375
Architecture: See Folk architecture
Asia Minor 089, 102, 126, 127, 131, 165, 188, 228, 234, 257, 258, 261, 405, 426, 427

Ballads 006, 010, 021, 026, 048, 068, 069, 099, 191, 242, 265, 297, 366, 396, 407. See also Folksongs
Beliefs 038, 041, 066, 111, 136, 137, 162, 167, 357. See also Collectanea; Ethnographic studies; Religion, Supernatural
Bibliographies 073, 108, 216, 254, 372, 402
Birth: See Pregnancy and childbirth

Charms 110, 142, 144. See also Collectanea; Folk medicine
Charon/Charos 009, 089, 092, 152. See also Death and the dead; Folksongs; Laments
Chios 013, 014, 015, 348, 349, 390
Christmas 057, 423. See also Holidays and festivals
Collectanea 002, 004, 013, 036, 037, 087, 118, 133, 154, 155, 164, 212, 266, 325, 339, 346, 373, 377, 378, 422, 430
Collections and archives 018, 060, 089, 090, 091, 093, 094, 095, 096, 097, 102, 108, 125, 126, 194, 203, 210, 215, 242, 244, 263, 276, 279, 282, 303, 304, 306, 323, 354, 378, 384, 394, 395, 396, 399. See also Folklore study.

Jokes: See Humor

Kalogheros 071, 083, 203, 230, 425
Kalymnos 343, 344, 345
Karaghiozis: See Shadow theater
Kataklysmos: See Holidays and festivals
Kephalonia: 022, 210, 243, 245, 424
Klephtic songs: See Ballads
Kos 378

Laments: See Death and the dead
Legends 034, 150, 196, 253, 330, 358, 364, 424. See
    also Folktales; Storytelling
Lesbos 133, 377

Macedonia 004, 072, 078, 169, 170, 221, 433. See
    also Anastenaria
Mantinadhes 176, 180, 198, 239, 342, 371, 391. See
    also Folksongs
Marriage 074, 165, 312, 411
Material culture 390
Matiasma 109, 135, 153, 181, 200, 260, 387, 417.
    See also Charms; Collectanea
Moirologhia 007, 008, 047, 054, 055, 058, 182, 317,
    388, 417 See also Charos; Death and the dead
Mumming: See Kalogheros; Ritual
Musical instruments 005, 060. See also Folk music

Names 039, 170, 253

Pregnancy and childbirth 329, 335, 336, 343
Proverbs 198, 248, 249, 250, 251, 258, 269, 324,
    363, 392. See also Collectanea
Puppet theater: See Shadow theater

Rebetika 052, 131, 190, 359, 408. See also Folk
    music
Religion 015, 137, 146, 167, 208, 231, 243, 245,
    257, 326, 341, 356, 389, 411. See also
    Anastenaria; Beliefs; Collectanea; Ritual
Rhodes: See Dodecanese Islands
Riddles: See Collectanea
Rites of passage 182, 400, 431. See also Death and
    the dead; Marriage; Pregnancy and childbirth